Dissent in American Religion

Chicago History of
American Religion

A Series Edited by
Martin E. Marty

Dissent in American Religion

Edwin Scott Gaustad

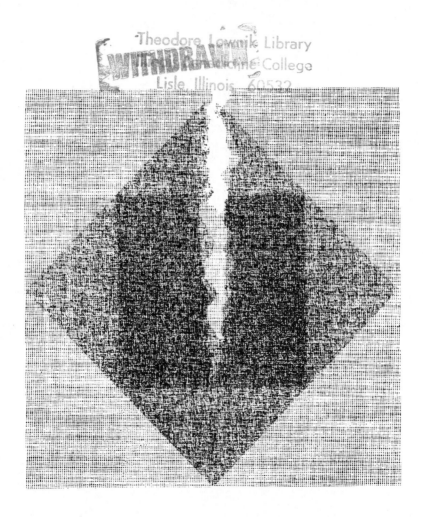

The University of Chicago Press   Chicago and London

The University of Chicago Press,
  Chicago 60637
The University of Chicago Press, Ltd.,
  London

International Standard Book
  Number: 0–226–28436–0
Library of Congress Catalog Card
  Number: 73–77131

EDWIN S. GAUSTAD is
professor of history at the University
of California, Riverside. His
previous books include *The Great
Awakening in New England, An
Historical Atlas of Religion in America*,
and *A Religious History of America*.
[1973]

*To my own children — and to
that unmoored student generation
of which they were a part;
together, they taught me more
about dissent than I really
wanted to know*

Contents

Foreword

As the United States approaches its bicentennial, its religious history can be reviewed in fresh ways. The disciplines in which the writing of that history occurred were originally nurtured in religious institutions. Thus most Roman Catholic history was written by Roman Catholics. It had to do with the stories of religious orders and dioceses or the biographies of bishops and founders. Jewish history usually took the form of chronicles designed for the Jewish community. Protestantism represented something of a special case, since Protestants outnumbered their co-religionists. They had such a great influence in shaping the public order that the impact of their points of view was not always restricted to their own ecclesiastical organizations.

When Protestantism still held a privileged position, however, it was difficult for historians to step back and look at the drama of American religious history in terms that transcended the norms of any particular group. By the middle of the twentieth century it had become clear to thoughtful Americans that a new situation was present. The old idea that white Protestantism represented a host culture and that others were more or less licit guests did not do justice either to the legal or spiritual realities of the nation's life.

The opportunity for new views came about in part because of the secularization of the discipline of religious history. Supreme Court decisions in 1962 and 1963 prohibited devotional exercises in public educational institutions. These were accompanied by fresh impetuses for the study of religion in those schools. Hundreds of public colleges and universities chartered such study. Inevitably, curiosity increased concerning the role religion had played in shaping national life. Distinguished leaders in the historical profession criticized the ways in which religious elements had been systematically screened out or subtly overlooked in the past.

Edwin Scott Gaustad's book on dissent and consent in American religion reflects the new perspectives that have developed during these years. He takes seriously the spokesmen for opposing points of view not from the aspect of a judge who knows what was best for America all along but as one who listens to thoughtful argument and understands the movement of power.

His topic also relates to a theme that developed during the years in which the study of religious history was being refined and relocated. This theme had to do with the role of consent and dissent themselves in the national script. For some time it was fashionable to divide historians into two camps. One group was purportedly committed to ideological defense of consensus in the American past. In this reading, the United States was a nation in which from the first citizens were almost predestined to converge on middles and golden means. The American environment itself predetermined the decisions people would make about conflict. They would tend to minimize ideology, downgrade doctrine, and stress practical adjustment to common-sense solutions.

Critics of this consensus school argued that the avoidance of ideology is itself an ideology. They said that historians of this stripe were themselves doctrinaires whose approach suppressed public interest in the dissenter, the outsider, the maverick, the revolutionary, and — most of all — the social groups or classes that did not accept the prevailing resolutions of American problems. Such criticism did serve to lift up for study some previously short-changed groups, among them members of minority groups

such as blacks. Their version of American history was being fresh-
ly studied, and it often turned out to have been in conflict with
that which earlier ruling groups had prescribed. Similarly, the
"consciousness-raising" activities of women's liberation movements inspired a generation of historians to take a second look
at what women were thinking and doing, and to find a somewhat
different version of the past on that basis. Some radical historians
claimed that whole social classes, particularly on the Left, had
been obscured from view by the established historians.

The debate over consensus and dissent inevitably spilled over
into the religious sphere, and may have helped occasion Professor
Gaustad's inquiry. If religion represents a realm in which men
and women try to come to terms with ultimate reality, a study
of that realm unquestionably will reveal something about other
decisions in life. Historians given to seeing conflict in the past
isolated black religious history, retold the story of the American
Indian's suppressed spiritual quest, or related religion to the
chronicle of social discontent. On the other side, those who pic-
tured Americans converging on a center stressed that religion
provided a kind of glue for an otherwise fragmenting society,
a lubrication for a social machinery that without it would have
ground to a halt.

Edwin Scott Gaustad's canvass of agreements and disagreements in the religious past suggests that neither ideological approach does justice to the way Americans organized themselves
religiously or how they looked at the world. Without question
they have engaged in many kinds of conflict over spiritual issues.
These conflicts have issued in the formation of new churches
and sects, the division of old ones, or intradenominational disputes of long standing. They have helped polarize citizens on
matters of public concern and inspire them to invoke the name
of God on issues about which they had made up their mind
long before the invocation. On the other hand, there has also
always been a counter-force that led them to restrain themselves,
and to suggest that the minor conflicts between ecclesiastics had

little or no import for the life of the whole society. America could be perceived as being "under God," while men could enjoy the luxury of debating finer theological points. "We are all in different ships heading for the same shore."

Conflict there has been, but when it was restricted to the internal life of religious groups, few were hurt. The American colonists and immigrants were often refugees from a Europe that had seen too many holy wars, and they would have nothing more to do with such ways of settling disputes. The nation was shaped in a period when a premium was placed on tolerance, and American believers rarely wanted to throw away such a hard-won value. It may occur to many readers of this book that the denomination itself was a rather clever invention designed to channel conflict into either creative or, at least, harmless directions. Religious dissent and conflict left few dead bodies.

The conflict that was expensive in terms of life and values went on largely outside the churches and synagogues. Whites often used religion to justify their removal of the American Indian from his historic domains, to legitimate human slavery on biblical grounds, to rationalize the ventures of their armies when North and South divided, to call down deity upon the adventures of political left or right. Religious defenses of contending positions in these volatile and often destructive encounters did heighten the motif of conflict in national life.

To say that religious conflict left few dead bodies is not to say that nothing of what went on in the denominational sphere is of much consequence in American history — anything but that. Professor Gaustad's study shows how seriously citizens have taken the debates over ultimate issues, how important these were for the ways they put their separate worlds together. It is clear that such debates are by no means to be relegated only to the past; the argument continues. It will be better informed as a result of inquiries such as Gaustad's.

Martin E. Marty
The University of Chicago

1

Prologue: A Delineation of Dissent

In America religious dissent is as vital as it is elusive. Like the secretions of the pituitary, the juices of dissent are essential to ongoing life even if we do not always know precisely how, when, or where they perform their task. And the not knowing — the flimsy, filmy elusiveness — is supremely characteristic of America's expressions of religious dissent. For in the United States no stalwart orthodoxy stands ever-ready to parry the sharp thrust or clever feints of dissent. No National Church resists or restrains the indigenous as well as the imported gift for schism. Of course, there are fashions, there are hucksterings of consent. Slogans do prevail for a time, and self-evident maxims receive widespread assent until another generation perversely fails to perceive their self-evidence. But the altars and idols revolve, court favorites fall, once noble churches stand in ruins, dogmas are defoliated and die. If only consensus stood still, dissent would be so much easier to locate, tag, and train.

That consensus — and society — do not stand still is the business and burden of dissent. All societies, even those that cry out against all change, require a mechanism for change. If the written law resembles that of the Medes and Persians, then there must be an oral law, a lively tradition, a juicier commentary, a freer oracle to make flexible and timely that which is "unchanging and eternal." All these mechanisms, however much a creature of the establishment they appear to be, hear and

respond to the strident, impatient voices of dissent. It is true
that societies often call for the silencing of dissent. Should a
society actually succeed, however, in suffocating all contrary
opinion, then its own vital juices no longer flow and the shadow
of death begins to fall across it. No society — ecclesiastical or
political, military or literary — can afford to be snared by its
own slogans.

Dissent, therefore, is not a social disease. While this proposition presents no particular difficulty when read in the library,
its reception is different in the marketplace or on the march,
in the town meeting or within the church council, at the political
forum or even around the family hearth. For dissent seen as
live action rather than as safe replay can be, and generally is,
irritating, unnerving, pig-headed, noisy, and brash. It can also
be wrong. And if often wrong, is not the suffering it provokes
too keen to compensate for its now-and-then stumble into the
right? That earnest, poignant question will not down. Its answer
determines how firm or fine that line between a society that
is open and one that is closed, a society that is virile and creative
as opposed to one that is sterile and decadent. To steal a rhythm
from Reinhold Niebuhr, consent makes democracy possible; dissent makes democracy meaningful.

In most of Western Civilization's history, religious dissent
has presented few problems of definition — whatever other problems it has brought in its wake. One recited the common creed
and counted the recalcitrants who refused to join in its intoning.
Or, one stood within the established church and readily
categorized all who were cast from that visible, much-favored
body. Or, one studied the law to see who enjoyed the sanction
and protection of public authority, and who did not. Dissent's
flag flew high, calling a few to its redoubt, warning more against
a treacherous, often fatal bog. Outcasts knew without question
of their despised and lowly estate; a few eccentrics may even
have reveled in it. The Establishment on the other hand bore

with dignity the burdens that leadership, power, and wisdom impose. Divisions were clear: the lions knew whom to devour.

The American experiment, the American folly, was to place both orthodoxy and dissent upon the same shifting platforms of public favor and public support. Throughout so much of American history, it has been distressingly difficult to separate the "ins" from the "outs": What was stubborn schism in Massachusetts was quiet conformity in Virginia; what was doctrinal sobriety in Pennsylvania was intolerable "enthusiasm" in Connecticut; what was proper churchmanship in Rhode Island was arrogant pretension almost everywhere else. E pluribus unum in early America? Hardly. Not only was there wild diversity in space, there was unsettling instability in time. The conformity so rigidly demanded in the seventeenth century was largely forgotten in the eighteenth. What was theological terror for one generation was for the next a vaguely disquieting dream. That which one age was willing to die for another age was not prepared to live for. And then deliberate disestablishment with the adoption of the First Amendment in 1791, further confounding the contrary categories of orthodoxy and dissent, or respectability and heresy, of decency and order against impropriety and sectarian novelty. The lions might be thirsty for blood, but where should they turn? So the confusions concerning good order, right opinion, and agreeable behavior continued until the vices of dissent were seen as virtues and the glories of pluralism were heralded as the American Way of Life. Up to a point.

For if society is diverse, flexible, adaptive, and pragmatic, why do we still hear quarrelsome cries of dissent? Why cannot everybody cooperate, get along, play the game, work within the system? Why multitudes still so unmelted, still so unwashed? Why the long lines of detractors and despisers, the sweaty crowds of nay-sayers and protesters? Is it possible that dissent is something more than flexible adaptability, that the abandonment of "creeds outworn" is not its full message? Is it possible to gain the "free world" and nonetheless lose one's soul? Dissent cannot be understood simply in terms of whines against oppression, resistance to organizational corruption, demurrers against the affirmations of others. To view dissent in these terms is to suppose that when all external restraints are removed and all ecclesiastical authority stilled, then dissent falls flat on its face never to rise again. This could be the case only if dissenters were merely noisy nay-sayers.

But history hones dissent to a fine edge: sharp, severe, unyielding. While it is true that restraint and oppression frequently give dissent its cohesion and therefore its strength as a mass movement, it is not true that, apart from these external forces, the dissenter is without aim or energy or nerve. Rather, the dissenter is a powerful if unpredictable engine in the service of a cause. Though he is prone to many sins, sloth is not his crime. The path of greatest resistance is frequently the very one that the dissenter sets himself upon. He may cast out demons dwelling in others; himself he cannot save.

One might argue that the above describes not the dissenting man but the religious man, *homo religiosus*. This observation has some validity. Religion in its essence is already offbeat, irregular, asymmetric. It confronts and attempts to cope with the unexpected and the unexplained. That which conforms, that which is balanced, that which is orderly and precise does not require the ministrations of cult or clergy, of ritual or myth. The profoundly religious man resists the routine, defies the machine, confounds the computer. In Abraham Heschel's terms, he is concerned not with process but with event. Yet, as everyone knows, religious institutions do make their peace with the world, they do themselves become part of the regular order. So the prophet contends against the priest, protests the accommodations, calls forth fresh energies, and challenges the unfeeling stones within existing structures. This reform of religion in the name of religion, this growing edge, this refusal to let well-enough alone, is the role of dissent. In Christian history even monasticism began as a form of dissent — a protest against a hardening of ecclesiastical arteries that even by the third century had already set in.

If dissent is a distillation of the religious quest, it may also be a manifestation of the unfettered human spirit. The dissenter is autonomous and inner-directed, displaying all of the pompous arrogance or heroic sacrifice of which a free spirit is capable. Like any fanatic, the dissenter can be a threat to civilization; like some fanatics, he may be the restorer or the inspirer of civilization. If cultural peaks are scaled only when a delicate balance between chaos and order obtains, dissent's contribution to one side of that balance is clear. The liberal, so often seen as the major instrument of progress and change, may in fact be the major voice for accommodation and consent. He sees the cultural train as something that all right-thinking persons should get aboard. The dissenter, on the other hand, may indicate that he really does not care for the way the tracks are laid, nor does he have much confidence that adjustments in throttle settings will give society a sense of direction or purpose. Long before counter-culture became a cliché, the dissenter was in the business of resisting a tyrannous majority, disturbing an establishment's peace, and breaking the bondage to a moderating, mollifying, debilitating civility.

In his *Genealogy of Morals*, Friedrich Nietzsche (1844–1900) vented his scorn upon a society grown soft and slavish. A political system, namely democracy, extols comfort, fashion, and mediocrity, while a religious system, namely Christianity, venerates meekness and reverence and all that is sickly and hanging on a cross. Together, he argued, they destroy the bold, free, creative spirit, replacing it with that "pink of modernity, who 'bites no longer,' shakes hands politely in a fashion that is at least instructive, the latter exhibiting a certain facial expression of refined and good-humored indolence, tinged with a touch of pessimism and exhaustion; as if it really did not matter to take all those things — I mean moral problems — so seriously."

What Nietzsche missed in the world around him was a spirit of dissent.

That same hollowness disturbed Sören Kierkegaard (1813–1855). With biting wit, the Danish theologian no less than the German philosopher was prepared to lay much blame at the door of the Christianity of his time and place. Kierkegaard's *Attack Upon "Christendom"* was, in the spirit of religious dissent, an attack upon a false, compromised, tame religion for the sake of a true, absolute, ever-discontented, ever-dissenting faith. The New Testament has nothing in common, he wrote, with all this "twaddle, twattle, patter, smallness, mediocrity, playing at Christianity, transforming everything into mere words." This is why in nineteenth-century Europe the New Testament seems unable "to punch a blow at real life." No one takes Christianity with sufficient seriousness even to attack it or dissent from it. ". . . for one certified hypocrite there are 100,000 twaddlers; for one certified heretic, 100,000 nincompoops." In this polite pink of modernity, one finds no absolute commitment, no unconditional surrender to a cause, but only a tentativeness, a pledge of trust "to a certain degree." This calculating caution is the disease that must be cured. If, however, the world sets about to cure itself, the chances are that it will seek to do so only "to a certain degree." A Swedish priest, Kierkegaard noted, dismayed by his sermon's effect on the congregation, added soothingly, "Children, do not weep; the whole thing might be a lie." Kierkegaard, too, missed the bold presence of dissent.

America, like nineteenth-century Europe, has had its theoreticians of dissent, but in far greater abundance has it had its practitioners. Dissenters against the structure and authority of ecclesiasticism, dissenters against the rigidity or folly or sterility of religious ideas, dissenters against the hopes and the messianic pretensions of the social order. Dissenters in such number and variety as to suggest that not all Americans surrendered to good-humored indolence or to mediocre twaddle. Not all resigned themselves to the awesome power of churches, of creeds, of cul-

tural captivities. Rather, they engaged in and took up the banner
of "dissent."

Still the word has not been neatly defined. It is easier to
describe where the wind blows and what effects it has than it
is to declare the precise nature of the wind. Dissent, we have
already observed, is elusive and erratic; religious dissent, far from
being an exception to that rule, is an exaggeration of it. Religious
dissent can be illustrated and typed; the "sins" against love,
against faith, against society can be described. All this, however,
is illustrative, not exhaustive. If it were possible totally to box
and compass religious dissent, its very character would be transformed. True dissent has too many moods, too many guises,
too many brief incarnations.

The enemy, on the other hand, is in a sense always the same:
Procrustean beds of any make, shibboleths in any form. Thus
the religious dissenter cries out against absurd confinements in
manners and morals, against the fatuous kowtowing of body
or of mind, against the circumscribing of vision or of aspiration,
against the evil that men do in the name of good, against indifference, insensitivity, and inertia. Sometimes the dissenter turns
out to be a saint, more often he does not. Sometimes he prevails,
more often he does not. Sometimes it is safe to ignore him,
more often it is not. Society's and religion's problem is that
amid the clanging cymbals of consensus it is frequently difficult
to hear what the dissenter is trying to say. One has to make
a special effort to listen. He that has ears to hear, said a dissenter
of ancient days, let him hear.

2

The Schismatics: Sinners Against Love

Western Christendom is no stranger to schism. Even that modifying "Western" points to the deep differences — historical, ecclesiastical, linguistic, theological, cultural — that set apart the Christianity of the patriarchs from the Christianity of the popes. The acrimony of A.D. 1054 only climaxed the centuries-long rift between Latin and Greek, between Rome and Constantinople. And as 1054 is a symbol of Christendom's deepest division, so Avignon is a symbol of the political turmoil and searing dissent within the Catholicism of the West. Popes and counter-popes, plots and counterplots, spoke not of a gospel of brotherhood and love but of factionalism and strife. The seamless robe of Christ was cut, torn, and badly patched.

The Council of Constance healed the visible wounds, but only for a moment. Then, later in the sixteenth century, all the wild passions of reformation and revolt broke loose. Old wounds were reopened as new ones were inflicted. He who does not have the Church for his Mother does not have God for his Father, Cyprian had long ago written. But for many dissenters at the dawn of a New Age, mother was a whore. Schism then became not a sin but a duty.

In bewildering and terrifying succession the cleavages came: Lutherans, Zwinglians, Calvinists, fanatic prophets, tender evangelicals, strange mystics, political opportunists, mediating scholars. Would the splintering of the Church (and therefore the shattering of society) never cease? Schism was, or so it seemed, a chain reaction. Once the "unity of the Church" (Cyprian again) was forsaken, once that loving loyalty was abandoned, obstinate divisiveness developed a momentum of its own. Like the scientists in Chicago splitting that first atom, who could know how — or if — it will ever end? If, moreover, the Church and the State are the warp and woof of all social order and of all cultural cohesion, what will happen when the threads of one begin to unravel? If love makes the Church one, what will hate do? Schism, at least in the sixteenth century, was scary business.

To be sure, many who denounced or departed from the visible Church of Saint Peter did so in the name of an invisible church of all the apostles. A catholic, apostolic, holy church of New Testament purity and of pre-Constantine simplicity — this was the end in view. And that of course was not schism, but reform. Saintly dissenters can turn from a corrupted tradition to a hallowed restoration. One can forsake the wilderness of the world to enter once more the carefully cultivated garden of Christ. Can all this be a sin against love? It can indeed, since when one leaves a household of faith, for whatever motive, the anguish of departure speaks of an injured or a suffering love. The mutual pain endured may even transmute that love into baser passion. The story of schism is, therefore, often a tragedy, seldom a comedy.

Of the Western world's many separations and schisms, America is the direct heir. European travelers to nineteenth-century America who expressed horror and dismay over America's sectarian jungle simply failed to recognize their own children. In many cases the children, having been ejected from home, did not care to recognize or greet the parent. Already identified as sinners against love, schismatics came from Switzerland and France, from Austria and Germany, from Britain and the Netherlands. Huguenots fled to Saint Augustine and to Charleston, Moravians to North Carolina and Pennsylvania, Mennonites and

Quakers to the Middle Colonies, Lutherans to Savannah, and
Pilgrims to Plymouth. Schism was, quite early, an American
way of life.

On the other hand, colonial America also received members
of the European establishment, notably from the national
churches of England, Holland, Sweden, Scotland, Germany, and
from the Church of Rome as well. Finding schism so rife, these
privileged churches sought to protect themselves from infection
by excommunication or exile, by persecution or persuasion, by
appeals to the authority of heaven and to the authorities back
home. Yet, the plague could not be checked. One by one, the
established ecclesiastical communities suffered defection and loss.
Even those who came to America as schismatics found in that
nonprivileged status no immunity from further schism. They
too endured challenges and bitter confrontations; they too
watched in sorrowful love as their own children left home. Several
aspects of the American scene made schism there a uniquely
lively, even attractive, option.

Piety

Piety places its first priority upon the direct, immediate, private,
incontrovertible experience of God. Not doctrinal declarations
but existential awareness, not ecclesiastical bureaucracies but
private epiphanies — these constitute the hard rock on which
religion must be built. "The pious," of either ancient Israel
or modern America, do not take too seriously the institutional
structures of religion. And in America, waves of pietism again
and again broke all over the farms, the hamlets, the towns.
That first momentous flood, the eighteenth century's Great
Awakening, left countless institutions shattered and clerical good
order permanently weakened. As the waters ebbed, new institutions and new ministries emerged from the soaked soil. For the
pietist generally broke from the old church only in order to
build a new one, one truer to his own rich experiences and

to those insights granted in the divine encounter. That new
church might fade in a few months or it might flourish indefi-
nitely. The not-yet-ended story of American religion offers ample
illustrations of both sorts of fate.

Isaac Backus (1724–1806), a member of Connecticut's Congregational church, broke from that official establishment to become — by patient, painful degree — a Massachusetts Baptist. As
a result of a conversion experience during the Awakening's pietistic flood, Backus found no satisfaction in the discipline and gov-
ernance of his parish church in Norwich. In 1748, along with
fifteen other fresh dissenters, Backus formed a New Light church,
this designation being indicative of strong support for that kind
of piety that the great revival seemed to represent. After an
eight-year struggle over the propriety of infant baptism, over
the exact nature of church government, and over the meaning
of the Lord's Supper, Backus organized a Baptist church in Mid-
dleborough, Massachusetts. Ordained as pastor of this newly
gathered flock in 1756, Backus continued in this capacity for
the remaining fifty years of his life.

Ardor cools and energetic zeal slows down. This is what has
happened to the New England Puritans, Backus contended; they
were pious men a century before, but sadly that piety had
declined. Their dissent had turned into consensus, their schism
into establishment. So the process had to be started over again:
corrupt Congregationalism must yield to a reincarnation of its
younger, purer self. Not schism, but restoration. In creating
a new Baptist church, Backus was only returning to the faith
and practice of "the first planters of New England . . .
excepting in the single article of sprinkling infants." And one
reason for rejecting that article was that the inclusion of infants
within the church tended to create a territorial or political
institution rather than a voluntary people of God. The church
is not a building, not an arm of government, but a gathering
of "saints and people by mutual acquaintance and communion,
voluntarily and understandingly covenanting and embodying

together for the carrying on the worship and service of God."
The people can only gather "understandingly" if they are themselves believers, converts, confessing adults — not infants
brought to baptism in the name of someone else's faith. When
the church is so constituted, then that visible and local institution begins to resemble that invisible and eternal Church of
Jesus Christ.

To preserve the spiritual purity of the church as well as to
protect the prerogatives of a sovereign God, Backus found it
necessary more than once to *Appeal to the Public for Religious
Liberty Against the Oppressions of the Present Day*. This tract, published in 1773, noted the irony of the American struggle for
civil liberty being carried on in the midst of the American (at
least New England) repression of ecclesiastical liberty. Com-
plaints of patriots against a tax on tea made sense to New England: why, then, did the dissenters' complaint against a tax on
behalf of "a ministry we cannot attend" make no sense to New
England's Standing Order? The ecclesiastical tax is far worse
than the tea tax, Backus asserted, for Americans can avoid the
latter by the simple expedient of not drinking tea. Dissenters,
however, cannot avoid the church tax regardless of what they
do; those who try to avoid it end up with their property con-
fiscated and themselves in jail. "But these lines are to let you
know," Backus wrote in 1774, "that we are determined not
to pay either [tax], not only upon your principle of not being
taxed where we are not represented, but also because we dare
not render that homage to any earthly power which I and many
of my brethren are fully convinced belongs only to God." Backus
called for nothing less than "liberty of conscience" — a liberty
that is inalienable because it derives not from men but from
God.

Years before the American Revolution Backus had confessed
that "Much of what I have written here I knew experimentally
before I did doctrinally." These are the purest words of pietism.
For it is in one's own experience that the profoundest meaning

is perceived and that authority for radical action is derived. If
the ecclesiastical establishment fails to speak out of or to human
experience, then that establishment must go. If one has been
radically altered in his life style and in his understanding by
the presence of a new Spirit within him, then much must be
changed. No longer can one endure a congregation of indifferent
members; no longer can one listen to lifeless, formal essays mas-
querading as sermons; no longer can one tolerate the unctuous
invasion of civil government into the most sacred recesses of
the human heart. No; new wine must not be poured into old
wineskins. New experiences made new saints, and new saints
needed a new church. So across New England schism followed
schism in the generation between the Great Awakening and the
American Revolution. So across America tiny scatterings of Baptists found themselves infused with new life. Fresh springs of
piety fed the denominational stream until in America it became
Protestantism's largest flow.

Liberty

Liberty unleashed gives schism a wide range. The American
Revolution and the lusty libertarianism that it incited gave broad
encouragement to those who found the British yoke not the
only restriction upon their freedom. Like the pious, the lovers
of liberty do not grant their highest priority to institutional
good order or to bureaucratic calm. James O'Kelly (1735–1826),
"full of democratic individualism and Irish passion," challenged
the tranquillity of America's newest denominational import:
Methodism. O'Kelly saw his church, though still young, as a
less than perfect imitator of the liberty that a new nation honored. He challenged Methodism to become less autocratic, less
authoritarian in its corporate life. His opponents such as Francis
Asbury saw the problem not in terms of autocracy but of anarchy.
How can a rapidly growing, widely scattered, ungainly adoles-
cent maintain in America any unity and order at all? For these

leaders the real question was whether Methodists were to be a Church or merely a brief meteoric light. Were Methodists to provide only a temporary frontier ministry, holding the line for Christianity until some "real" church with real sacraments appeared on the scene?

Scarcely had the Revolution ended when representatives of some fifteen thousand Methodists in the new nation gathered in Baltimore in 1784 for the famous "Christmas Conference." At that important meeting, a creed was approved, a "Sunday Service" book was adopted, a discipline was modified, and a salary scale for circuit riders was set. On Christmas Day itself, Francis Asbury, still a layman, was ordained a deacon; the next day he was ordained an elder, and the next day a superintendent or bishop. For this newly formed Methodist Episcopal church, it was a rapid escalation in office and in authority. Many Methodists, recalling too well the imperious bishops of England's Church, feared that newly won liberties, civil and ecclesiastical, were threatened.

In 1792, therefore, a General Conference of American Methodists was called, partly to ward off a growing centralization and an increasingly unchallenged exercise of episcopal powers. Drawing preachers from all along the Atlantic seaboard, that conference debated at length the nature and extent of authority within their church — a durable ecclesiastical concern. In the course of that debate, Methodism even in the rosy flush of youth confronted and suffered schism. O'Kelly, an effective, popular evangelist in Virginia, found himself lifted by and swept along in the spirit of the nation's new liberties. To what man was an American prepared to surrender these liberties? To none, replied O'Kelly, not even to a brother in Christ. "It is not our superior wisdom, nor ignorance, that renders us so ungovernable, but our invariable determination to stand fast in our civil and religious liberties 'wherein God hath strangely made us free'." In the context of governing a denomination, what did such grand sentiments mean? For O'Kelly they meant, at least, that a

bishop's right to determine where each minister should work
was a limited right. They meant, at least, that a mere, ordinary
preacher (but an American nonetheless) had the right of appeal
from a decision that could be mere whimsy or caprice. In 1790
O'Kelly had observed in some dismay: "I now began to discover
the rapid five years growth of 'a moderate Episcopacy.' Where-
unto shall I liken it? It is like a dwarf whose head grows too
fast for its body."

The conference agreed to consider that hard question of autocracy versus anarchy. The form in which that question was put
was a motion for debate: "After a bishop appoints the preachers
at conference to their several circuits, if any one thinks himself
injured by the appointment, he shall have liberty to appeal to
the conference and state his objections; and if the conference
approve his objections, the bishop shall appoint him to another
circuit." What might seem like a modest proposal precipitated
intense theological and emotional contention. "The arguments
for and against the proposal were weighty," reported Methodism's early historian Jesse Lee, adding that "there had
never been a subject before us that so fully called forth the
strength of the preachers." O'Kelly and his backers argued that
the New Testament knew no such ambitious powers as those
exercised by Asbury, that recently emancipated Americans should
not now become "slaves to ecclesiastical oppression," and that
Methodists were "far gone into popery." After three full days
of debate the vote was counted: O'Kelly and friends had lost.
The next morning, writes Lee, when the conference reassembled,
O'Kelly sent a letter indicating that "they could no longer sit
among us." Efforts to prevent a serious, permanent fracture were
of no avail. Jesse Lee watched as O'Kelly and others went to
get their horses; as they rode off Lee remarked to a friend standing
nearby that he was sorry to see "that old man" — O'Kelly was
fifty-seven years of age at the time — "go off in that way, for
I was persuaded that he would not be quiet long, but he would
try to be head of some party."

The prophecy proved correct. Despite conference overtures to
O'Kelly to pay him his annual salary, "provided he was peaceable
and forbore to excite divisions among the brethren," defection
came. Large numbers of Methodists in Virginia and North
Carolina came together to create the Republican Methodist
church. "Republican" because it was open and democratic, with
clergy and laity occupying virtually the same plane of authority.
Unlike the parent body, however, it was not an "Episcopal"
church, for this word connoted all that rigid authoritarianism
and unwarranted presumption which the new church meant to
avoid. "If Christians are free citizens of Zion," wrote O'Kelly,
"they should prize those liberties, seeing they were purchased
with the precious blood of Christ." If Asbury wished to be a
pope, let him proceed. But also let him know that some Americans do not propose to exchange a British slavery or a Roman
prelacy for a latter-day variety of tyranny. As thousands rallied
to O'Kelly's republican cause, Asbury confided to his diary (24
March 1793): "I have no time to contend, having better work
to do; if we lose some children God will give us more."

Asbury's confidence was also vindicated. The Methodist Epis-
copals grew mightily while the Methodist Republicans within
a decade lost their distinctive thrust. By 1801 O'Kelly's group
had become just another modest experiment in shaping an
ecclesiastical society without rule, without hierarchy, without
creed. Adopting the less revealing name of the "Christian
church" ("suppose we dissolve [all] unscriptural names, and for
peace's sake, call ourselves Christians"), the O'Kelly faction
merged with other schisms led by Vermont's Abner Jones and
by Kentucky's Barton Stone. This loosely organized communion
survived until 1931 when it was absorbed by the one-time prince
of establishmentarianism: New England's Congregational
churches.

Some schisms, such as that in which Isaac Backus participated,
succeed beyond all dreams. Many more, such as that led by
James O'Kelly, fall short of all hopes. Asbury concluded, "After

all Satan's spite, I think our shifting and shaking will be for good." For Americans in the first generation of nationhood, this was a sensible, supportive position to adopt. How else might one endure the slings and pains, the turmoils and confusions, found in such abundance among the blessings of liberty?

Frontier

In the colonial period all America was a frontier. As such it suffered the scorn of a more cultured, self-consciously cosmopolitan Europe — a Europe that delighted in pointing out the New World's general inferiority as well as its cultural vacuity. Where were America's great artists, poets, musicians, philosophers? Eventually these questions, themselves rather vacuous, were either refuted or withdrawn. And in time the colonial cities — Boston, Newport, New York, Philadelphia, Charleston — did spawn a culture and did boast a civilization. In the nineteenth century, however, the tension between barbarism and culture, between nature and civilization, was a staple of the American diet along the advancing frontier.

"Frontier spirit" seems a more acceptable term than "barbarism" in explaining that tension to ourselves. Nature instilled within the western settler that independence and hardihood, that self-reliance and individualism, which a distant and more effete society might disdain. At least in retrospect the "frontier spirit" appeared more asset than liability. In the days when trails were blazed and trees felled, however, the tension is there: the embarrassment or contempt of "culture" when confronted by the rude, ill-mannered, unlettered bumpkin; contrariwise, the irritation or disdain of "nature" in the presence of the haughty, meticulous, helpless urbanite. In religion, that tension expressed itself in many ways: quarrels over proper form, pure doctrine, cold formalism, good order, wild enthusiasm, and especially the nature and function of the ministry. Given the limitations and challenges of life on the frontier, the role of the clergy was often seen in a different, forest-filtered light. And because that role was not identical with its urban counterpart, the necessity for all the urban world's cultural accoutrements was seriously questioned. Now and again it was even hinted that culture was the enemy of godliness.

The Cumberland River flows west from the Cumberland Mountains of Kentucky and Tennessee, then turns north into the Ohio River not far from the junction of that river with the mighty Mississippi. The Cumberland River created a fertile valley; the frontier religion there did the same. Cumberland country produced an impressive crop of revivals, itinerant preachers, ecclesiastical wrangles, and lush denominational growth. Within Presbyterianism, this Cumberland frontier promoted yet another schism — Europe's horror so swiftly becoming America's commonplace. Of the several factors involved in forming the Cumberland Presbyterian church in 1810, the frontier was directly or indirectly responsible for all. The schismatics were strongly pro-revivalist: the frontier demanded immediate, demonstrable results. The schismatics were jealous of their own ecclesiastical privileges and prerogatives: the frontier lowered one's tolerance for externally imposed authority. Further, the schismatics rejected doctrine that seemed too intricately reasoned, too far-fetched or abstruse: the frontier favored common sense. (As one sympathizer noted, "God never called us to scholasticism. Writing theodicies is not in our commission. Working for souls with all our forces is.") Finally, the dissident party refused to place a higher premium upon formal clerical education than upon clear evidence of "extraordinary talents and piety": the frontier thrived upon experience.

The lives of certain young men set apart for a fruitful frontier ministry reveal all four of these tensions between nature and civilization. Cumberland Presbytery said that these young men were pious and called of God; Synod of Kentucky, the higher echelon of authority, said that these men were illiterate and doctrinally unsound. Presbytery said that the glorious successes

of the revivals validated their ministry; Synod warned against
those "extravagant and indecent outrages" that validate nothing.
Presbytery protested that Synod had no right whatsoever to take
action against ministers whom Presbytery had licensed and
ordained, such action being "illegal, unconstitutional, null and
void"; Synod, not surprisingly, found otherwise.

One of the dissidents around whom the theological torrents
swirled was Finis Ewing (1773–1841). A native of Virginia,
a youthful Ewing moved to Cumberland country where he was
licensed to preach in 1802, the year that Cumberland Presbytery
was formed. Within two years, Cumberland Presbytery has "licensed to exhort" some seventeen young men, none of whom
(it appeared) had been required to accept the Westminster Con-
fession of Faith nor had their educational qualifications for en-
trance into the ministry been established. What was to Presbytery
a mere reordering of priorities was to Synod a scandal and an
offense. Having "received full satisfaction of the good moral
character" of one of the seventeen young men, having learned
of "his experimental acquaintance with religion, his knowledge
of divinity, having also given good specimens of his ability and
usefulness in the church as a public exhorter," Cumberland Presbytery did proceed to "license him to preach the gospel of Christ
within their bounds or wherever God in his providence may
call him." The issue was joined: in setting apart a man for the
ministry, were morality and piety and oratory enough?

In 1805 Synod of Kentucky established a commission to investigate the propriety of what Cumberland Presbytery had already
done and was continuing to do. It was hard to believe, Ewing's
biographer wrote, that "a set of Presbyterian ministers . . .
could oppose a genuine revival of religion, ridicule evangelical religion, and remonstrate against the licensure of pious
and intelligent young men whose labors were specially needed
and prayed for by the destitute congregations." It was no doubt
even harder to believe that Synod would then actually dissolve
Cumberland Presbytery and prohibit the clergy whom it had

licensed from preaching or administering the sacraments "until they submit to our jurisdiction and undergo the requisite examination." Ewing and others, refusing to accept this synodical command, formed a council in order to carry their protest to Presbyterianism's highest authority in America: the General Assembly.

In 1807 the aggrieved party presented a long letter to the assembly, detailing what great things God was doing in Cumberland valley, and what greater victories over Satan lay ahead if only certain evil men were rebuked and restrained. Revivals, breaking out all over the western frontier, brought hundreds and hundreds of concerned men and women, even "deists, drunkards, Sabbath-breakers and all the different characters that compose the great class of the wicked." As a result, revivalism which spread "like a rapid flame," greatly enlarged the kingdom of God on earth.

Now, truly the harvest was great and the laborers few. Unable to resist the pressing solicitations from every quarter for preaching, with unutterable pleasure we went out, laboring day and night, until our bodies were worn down, and after all we could not supply one-third of the places calling upon us for preaching. While thus engaged, and the gracious work still going on, we observed what was very remarkable, that in almost every neighborhood there was some one who appeared to have uncommon gifts for exhortation and prayer, and were zealously engaged in the exercises thereof, while the Lord wrought by them to the conversion of many. Viewing the infant state of the church in our country, the anxious desire for religious instruction, the gifts, diligence, and success of those we have mentioned, and the scriptural authority for exhortation, we were induced . . . to open a door for the licensure of exhorters. . . . It was now agreed that any of those who might be licensed, and manifested extraordinary talents and piety, should be considered as candidates for the ministry . . .

From our personal knowledge of those men's good talents, piety, and usefulness; from the numerous warm petitions of the people at large — from the example of many Presbyteries — from the silence of scripture on literary accomplishments — from your own declaration . . . "That human learning is not essential to the ministry" — from

the exception made in the book of discipline in extraordinary cases;
we humbly conceived, that it would not be a transgression either of
the laws of God or the rule of the church, to license men of such description. We therefore did license them, and a few others at different
times afterward: some of them with and some of them without literary acquisitions; but all men of gifts, piety and influence . . .
Now, the work of the Lord went on.

The case for the defense had been strongly put. Do not listen,
argued the frontier party, to the "opposing brethren" who grossly
misrepresent "our characters, our conduct and the doctrine we
taught." Restore to us our freedoms and "our Presbyterial rights,
never forfeited, but wrested from us." The General Assembly,
having heard all, decided that enough merit could be found
at least to ask Synod of Kentucky to review its entire handling
of the matter and report back to the assembly. Synod reviewed
its former judgments, found nothing wanting, and reported as
much to the next meeting of the assembly. At this juncture,
the assembly supported its synod, leaving Ewing and his fellow
frontier revivalists with no recourse except schism or submission.
On 4 February 1810, Ewing and others reestablished the dis-
solved, discredited Cumberland Presbytery. In so doing, they
created a new church. That new church, unlike the old, would
recognize that the American frontier had requirements and
urgencies of its own; to ignore "the peculiar state of our country"
with its peculiar needs in discipline, doctrine, and vocation was
folly indeed.

As is repeatedly the case in America's religious history, schism
was not deliberately sought. On the contrary, Ewing's council
had for five years carefully avoided being anything other than
a "council," having no desire "to become a new party, nor to
produce a secession in the church." By 1810, however, all alternatives had been foreclosed and every doubt, said Ewing, "was
entirely banished." When that definitive action was finally taken,
it hardly deserved to be called schism since only four clergymen
left the parent body for the new church. Ninety per cent of the

new church's membership, moreover, was "made up of converts won from Satan's dominion and not of proselytes from other churches." Drawing from Satan's dominion, which at times seemed identical with the frontier, the Cumberland Presbyterian church by the end of the century had acquired a membership of nearly two hundred thousand. Six years into the twentieth century, the majority of the church reversed its schismatic direction and returned to the parental household. The "peculiar state of our country" in 1906 called for still different understandings of man's vocation in God's world.

Evangelicalism

In 1843 Robert Baird published his *Religion in America*, the first major survey of what was to be an increasingly baffling pattern of ecclesiastical diversity. To a non-American audience the pattern was especially bewildering. True, said Baird in addressing his British readers, the denominations are many, the variety is luxuriant, the novelty is apparent. Yet, if one looks beneath all the superficial differences and organizational labels, he will discover only two basic kinds of religion in America: evangelical and nonevangelical. For Baird, these categories were both significant and distinct. Evangelical religion — clearly his preference — is that which emphasizes the Church's ministry of salvation. Above all else Christianity is a message of Christ's atoning death, a message that God was in Christ reconciling the world unto Himself. The Church may do other things; it may be other things; but if it is evangelical it will see its prime task always as that of saving souls. These "Churches whose religion is the Bible, the whole Bible, and nothing but the Bible" must therefore be distinguished from "all those sects that either renounce or fail faithfully to exhibit the fundamental and saving truths of the Gospel." It is characteristic of these nonevangelical churches that they honor tradition more than scripture and instruct more than convert; they in fact introduce "another Gospel."

Having made his categories, Baird confidently fills them. The evangelicals include Presbyterians (his own denomination), Congregationalists, Baptists, Methodists, Dutch Reformed, Moravians, Quakers, and Episcopalians. The nonevangelicals — and Baird granted that they had little in common except that "none can be associated with the evangelical Protestant churches"— included Roman Catholics, Unitarians, Universalists, Swedenborgians, Jews, Mormons, deists, and others. Even among the evangelicals, however, classification had some ambiguity. Suppose that within a single denomination one has both evangelical and nonevangelical strains? Suppose that in this tug-of-war the common cord to which all communicants are holding suddenly snaps? In a situation such as that, the "evangelical" thrust can itself become a cause of schism.

In the Protestant Episcopal church in the United States, tension and strain have regularly been a way of life. A via media steering between the Catholic and Protestant poles, the Church of England like its American counterpart braced itself against steady and contrary tugs. Occasionally, something would give. In the England of the 1830s and 1840s the Oxford Movement, under the eloquent leadership of John Henry Newman, gave a sudden jerk in the direction of pre-Reformation Catholic tradition. When in 1845 Newman himself along with hundreds of his countrymen became Roman Catholics, the schism seemed so severe as to threaten that via media itself. Though shaken, the Church of England withstood a powerful pull in one direction.

In America the tug was in the opposite direction, partly in clear reaction against the tendencies and consequences of the Oxford Movement. Concern about the "Romanizers and ritualists" led many Episcopalians to an emphatic assertion that theirs was a *Protestant* Episcopal church. The Civil War delayed the American reaction to England's ecclesiastical strain, but soon after that war ended, this country's Episcopal communion found itself teetering on the edge of schism, found itself "passing through a crisis — solemn, momentous, awful."

In those words Bishop George David Cummins (1822–1876) warned of the "deep, widespread effort to eliminate from the Church her distinctively Reformed or Protestant character, and to place her where she stood before the Reformation, defiled by the corruption of mediaeval times." Earnestly he inquired whether America's Episcopalians would "resist the mighty tide of error in our midst tending towards Rome"? Would they stand together on the "great platform of Evangelicism"? Or would they permit themselves to forget the martyrdoms and sacrifices of the sixteenth century, being distracted and seduced by altars and superaltars, by crosses and candlesticks, by genuflections and crossings, by chasubles, maniples, albs, and birettas, and worst of all by "the avowed belief in the 'real presence' and 'baptismal regeneration' "? Had Robert Baird properly categorized the Episcopal Church in America — evangelical or not?

Cummins, consecrated bishop in Louisville in 1866, received his episcopal dignity with pride: "I am the eighty-first in the order of succession of American bishops." For such a man, conscious of his churchmanship, committed to historical continuity and sacred tradition, honored by his peers, schism would not come easily. The path of the schismatic was hard, painful, offensive, and at almost all costs to be avoided. Yet it is the path that Bishop Cummins walked shortly after his elevation.

Together with other evangelical bishops, or "bishops of the evangelical school," Cummins endeavored to correct the "errors" creeping into the church's liturgy and doctrine. At the General Convention meeting in New York in 1868, however, he decided that the mood was against him. If changes were made in the canonical legislation at that meeting, they were more likely to be made away from rather than toward the evangelical position. So swiftly did the current run toward the Oxford Movement that pressing for any kind of vote seemed unwise. "All that we can do," wrote a Bishop Cummins who had no desire to see schism rip his church apart, "is to plant ourselves upon the

Prayer Book as it is, for thus we can save any movement *Romeward* or *Greekward* . . ." If we can stand fast, we can still keep this mediating church "upon the platform of the Reformation." Or so it seemed in 1868; a mere five years later that hope was shattered.

In those brief bitter years the plunge toward schism was deepened by frictions in personality as well as in principle. In order to further the evangelical cause, Cummins as assistant bishop of Kentucky "invaded" the diocese of Henry J. Whitehouse, bishop of Illinois. Whitehouse registered his "solemn protest against acts and temper so derogatory to the dignity of our office," explicitly restraining Cummins "against your visiting my diocese to officiate in any manner within its bounds." The itinerant Cummins nonetheless journeyed to Chicago's Trinity Church, explaining that he was merely doing what any simple clergyman could do: namely, accept "an invitation from the rector of any church to preach to his people and ask for contributions from them in behalf of any lawful Church work. This right I have not lost by becoming a bishop . . ."

Other bishops "of the evangelical school" supported Cummins, though some urged moderation in both his language and his behavior. But moderation was not to Cummins's taste, especially as it appeared to him that tyranny in his Church was on the rise. "There are a good many Hildebrands on both sides of the Atlantic in this nineteenth century." Cummins accepted with alacrity the invitation to address the Evangelical Alliance, gathering in New York City in 1873, for here was a forum worthy of his broad sympathies. No narrow denominationalist, he wished to embrace evangelicals of every persuasion, not simply those who happened to be Episcopalians. Nothing in Episcopal order, he noted, prohibits "an act of inter-communion among Christian people who are one in faith and love," nor does the Church of England "deny the validity of the orders of ministry of the non-Episcopal churches." This was more than sympathy; it was subversion.

Evangelicalism at that point struck out, not only among the High Church Romanizers but also among many Low Church Protestantizers formerly in Cummins's camp. Reluctantly but inevitably, Cummins took that further fated step. "I have lost all hope," he wrote his own bishop in 1873, "that this system of error, now prevailing so extensively in the Church of England and in the Protestant Episcopal Church in this country, can be or will be eradicated by any action of the authorities of the Church, legislative or executive." The only way to save that dear church, he added, is to so revise its prayer book as to eliminate "all that gives countenance, directly or indirectly, to the whole system of Sacerdotalism and Ritualism." Such reform, he sadly admitted, was not about to take place given the existing structures and sentiments of the Protestant Episcopal church in the United States. "I therefore leave the Communion in which I have labored in the sacred ministry for over twenty-eight years, and transfer my work and office to another sphere of labor."

That "other sphere" was the Reformed Episcopal church, formed on 2 December 1873, less than a month after the letter quoted above was written. Meeting in the YMCA in New York, the new fellowship returned to the prayer book of 1785 — an earlier, less Romanizing time. Affirming its full faith in and reliance upon the Holy Scriptures, the Reformed church rejected those "erroneous and strange doctrines" that are "contrary to God's Word." These include the notion that only one form of church government is acceptable to God as well as the pretension that "priests" enjoy some special priesthood beyond that in which all true believers are found. Furthermore, the Lord's table is just that — not an altar — and Christ is present in the Lord's Supper not by virtue of the bread and wine. Finally, baptism and regeneration are not "inseparably connected." If the new church could not demolish "the whole system of Sacerdotalism and Ritualism," it could at least begin that great work.

The work proved too great. By 1877 the Reformed Episcopal church had some five thousand communicants and about twice

that number at the turn of the century. The high point had
been reached, however, and a gradual decline set in thereafter.
In 1970, the new church had a membership of less than 1 percent
of that belonging to the old church. In the eyes of the larger
fellowship, not a substantial schism. In the eyes of the smaller
communion, not a schism at all. For, as the organizers of the
Reformed church sought to make clear, it was the Protestant
Episcopal Church that was torn by strife, schism, confusion,
and faction. That church included "Low, High, High and Dry,
High, fancy, mixed and compound." Such a description "does
not exaggerate the schismatic condition" of the parent body.
To separate from a church so impure "is not only Gospel, but
it is common sense." And if schism per se be a sin, separation
from schism is nothing less than an apostolic duty.

Ethnicity

In all of American life the ethnic pull reveals an awesome
strength. Certain "unmeltable ethnics" fade from view only temporarily, while other ethnics that the nation hardly knew it pos-
sessed surge forward. So powerful is this pull in American religion that, at one time or another, it has overridden theology,
shaped the liturgy, shattered or refashioned the polity. The Evangelical and Reformed Church, for example, came into being in
1934 in recognition that a common background of German pietism unified the two constituent bodies more than their theological divergence separated them. Or, to cite another example,
Lutheranism in America while more or less united theologically
segregated itself ecclesiastically along purely ethnic lines: Swedish, Finnish, Danish, Norwegian, Icelandic, German. Scottish
Presbyterians — the Covenanters and the Seceders — found
unity difficult with British Presbyterians or even with Scotch-
Irish. German Baptists — the Dunkers or the Brethren —
shared little with the larger Baptist groups or either British or
African background. Mennonites from Russia seldom joined with
Mennonites from Switzerland, and German Jews worshipped

apart from Jews emigrating out of Eastern Europe. None of this amounted to schism, for no parent church existed. But ethnicity created divisions that Scripture hardly authorized and that Americanization only at length was able to heal.

All these divisions and difficulties, however, scarcely compared with the ethnic complexities confronting ancient Christianity, Eastern and Western. The Eastern Orthodox emigration to America, largely a twentieth-century one, presented a brilliant mosaic of ethnic coloration; Bulgarian, Romanian, Albanian, Serbian, Syrian, Ukranian, Russian, and Greek. Since these groups worshipped in national churches in the homelands, they naturally expected to maintain the same national, cultural, ethnic ties in America. For the most part, they have done just that, Americanization still being a generation or two away for most of these immigrants. In Roman Catholicism, on the other hand, a central papal authority maintained or at least fought for an ecclesiastical loyalty that transcended political and ethnic divisions. In the United States pressure grew among German, French, Irish, Italian, and, much later, Mexican-American for separate church structure and recognition. Despite the relentless agitation and the often persuasive argumentation, the Roman Catholic church resisted these centrifugal forces. Ethnicity must not mock or destroy catholicity. In this cause, Roman Catholicism was earnest, persistent, and almost successful.

Near the end of the nineteenth century, in Scranton, Pennsylvania, a segment of the Polish population challenged the Roman unity. To the Poles, it appeared that they were rejecting not catholicity but only another form of ethnicity: namely, the Irish. The Polish parishioners of the Sacred Heart of Jesus found themselves ruled not by a Polish but by an Irish bishop, governed not by a Polish but by an Irish mayor, outvoted even in local parish affairs by "foreign priestly power." Discontent grew to such an extent that riots broke out in the 1890s and aggrieved laymen looked somewhere, anywhere, for help. Counsel and comfort was sought from a former Scranton priest and dedicated Pole, Francis Hodur (1866–1953). Hodur's counsel was direct: "Let all those who are dissatisfied and feel wronged . . . set about organizing and building a new church, which shall remain in possession of the people themselves. After that, we shall decide what further steps are necessary."

The steps that proved necessary led steadily toward schism. First, the parish church was built, the Polish laity providing the funds and the labor. Second, the bishop (Irish) was invited to bless the new church and appoint a pastor. Third, the bishop declined to do either until the property was transferred to him. Fourth, the parish church decided that its turn to decline had come. Naming their parish Saint Stanislaus, in honor of Poland's bishop and martyr, they acclaimed their church "the first free Polish National parish in the world" and called Francis Hodur to be their first pastor. Assuming this pastoral office in 1897, Hodur sailed to Rome the next year to argue for a special ecclesiastical structure for Poles in America, a structure that would grant greater authority to the laity, greater ethnic solidarity to the new immigrants. He lost his case, and in October 1898 he and his parishioners were excommunicated. Two years later, the Scranton parish celebrated America's first mass in the Polish language.

Scranton was not alone in the ethnic struggle. In Buffalo, in Chicago, in various cities along the eastern seaboard, other Polish enclaves found themselves similarly distressed. In 1904, delegates from five states assembled in Scranton to establish the Polish National Catholic Church in America. Representing a membership of about fifteen thousand, this ethnic schism took its constitutional cue from the Saint Stanislaus parish that had contended from the beginning that "the church properties are to be owned and controlled by the people . . ." Francis Hodur, named as bishop-elect of the new church, was consecrated in Utrecht by the Old Catholic Church — itself a European schism arising from the pronouncement of papal infallibility at Vatican Council I in 1870.

The American schism, the only permanent one that the Roman Catholic Church in the United States has suffered, grew from its initial fifteen thousand to a membership two decades later of about sixty thousand. By mid-century the number of adherents had reached one-quarter million, suggesting that this schism will survive. It will survive, that is, so long as ethnicity is a central concern. And ethnicity, rather than doctrine or experience or ecclesiology, initially distinguished this Polish church. In 1908 a Polish National Union, formed in Scranton, augmented the services that a purely ecclesiastical organization could render. Hand in hand, the union and the church forged strong ethnic bonds among the Poles. The church included in its calendar festivals as much national (i.e., Polish) as they were religious. Polish newspapers, Polish magazines, Polish annual gazettes appeared under the church's auspices. And the language of worship, public or private, was consistently, proudly Polish. With the establishment of the Polish Republic in 1919, the American church even authorized a mission program in the home country.

Yet, not all of the development of the Polish National Catholic Church followed predictable ethnic lines. The Word of God "heard and preached" was soon elevated to the status of a sacrament. In 1921, celibacy was no longer required of the parish priest. In 1946 in a clearly trans-cultural gesture the Polish church and the Episcopal church acknowledged the validity of each other's ministries and sacraments. The Polish church has also participated in such broadly ecumenical ventures as the National and the World Council of Churches. Ethnic identity, moreover, has not prevented these Poles from accepting Lithuanians, Slovaks, and others into their fellowship. Finally, if this Polish church is not all-Polish, it must also be noted that not all Polish Catholics are included in its ranks. Indeed, the vast majority of America's Poles remain within the Roman Catholic Church. Catholicity is, after all, only lightly mocked.

Race

The schisms over slavery before the Civil War are well known: the denominational travail that wracked all American religion was most dramatically evident among Baptists, Methodists, and Presbyterians. Each of these national bodies split in two in the 1840s and 1850s; a century later the deepest wounds had scarcely begun to heal. But these great separations dealt not so much with race as they did with the institution of slavery itself. Debates raged over its moral status as a human institution, its economic status as an agricultural necessity, its political status as a continuing option for the states. As white contested against white, the hard lines of division — geographical, not racial — were drawn.

Both before that war, however, and in far larger numbers after, separations came along lines that were unmistakably racial. Richard Allen, weary of white presumption, formed an African Methodist Society in Philadelphia in 1787. In New York City, another Methodist group withdrew in 1796 along lines that were racial. The wholesale separation of blacks from the predominantly white churches is, however, a postwar phenomenon. Among the Baptists, where the greatest number of black Christians are to be found, the schisms on the grounds of race are of special importance.

Virtually the only door open to the nineteenth-century black male for social or economic advancement was the Christian ministry. In the laissez-faire church polity of the Baptists, furthermore, the black clergyman found himself relatively free of white supervision and control, completely free of white bishops or of tight hierarchical structure. This latitude, together with the open spontaneity of Baptist worship, white or black, helped move Negroes into Baptist ranks with frequency and ease. At the end of Reconstruction in 1877 Negro Baptists numbered at least six hundred thousand, a total that increased to well over a million by the end of the century. A mere two generations later the number of Negro Baptists was an astounding nine million.

Yet, even with the lax ecclesiastical structures of the Baptists, even in the midst of the alleged color blindness of Christian theology, the spectre of race arose — and would not disappear. It was impossible to ignore "the stern realities of the situation," to use Carter G. Woodson's phrase. Those unpleasant realities included an unequal treatment of Negro pastors and an unflattering approach to Negro scholars within the broad denominational family. The pill turned too bitter to swallow when in the 1890s the white-dominated American Baptist Publication Society withdrew its earlier invitation to black Baptist scholars — graduates of Brown, Bucknell, Andover-Newton, etc. — to contribute articles for the society's regular publications. While whites could write for both blacks and whites, blacks, it was decided, could write religious literature used only by blacks. The society's decision, wrote Lewis G. Jordan, sent a "a wave of sorrow, disappointment, and resentment to the very finger tips of all organizations among Negro Baptists."

In 1895, representatives of three Negro Baptist organizations (Baptist Foreign Mission Convention, organized in 1880; American National Baptist Convention, organized 1886; and National Baptist Education Convention, organized 1893) met in Atlanta, Georgia, to form a single national body for all black Baptists. The resulting National Baptist Convention differed from the parent body in neither theology nor polity — only in race. The Reverend E. K. Love of Savannah, Georgia, and formerly an agent for the American Baptist Publication Society, defined the issue clearly in 1896. Speaking to a national gathering in Saint Louis, Love observed that the time had come for Negro pastors and Negro writers to go their own way.

As closely connected and as affectionately attached to the American Baptist Publication Society as I am, I could not be so disloyal as to rebel against my race and denomination. . . . I am a loyal Baptist and a loyal Negro. I will stand or fall, live or die, with my race and denomination . . . There is as strong an argument in favor of a distinctive Negro Publishing House as there is for distinctive Negro churches, schools or families. It is just as reasonable

and fair for Negroes to want these things to themselves as it is for
white people to want them to themselves. If one is necessary and
right, the other is equally so. It never was true anywhere, and perhaps
never will be, that a Negro can enjoy every right in an institution
controlled by white men that a white man can enjoy. There is not as
bright and glorious a future before a Negro in a white institution as
there is for him in his own. It cannot be denied that we can better
marshal our forces and develop our people in enterprises manned by
us. We can more thoroughly fill our people with race pride, denominational enthusiasm and activity, by presenting to them for their
support enterprises that are wholly ours.

Stern realities called for schism. The National Baptist Convention (NBC) quickly enlarged the scope of its activities as a new
denomination. Under its first president, E. C. Morris (1855–
1922), the NBC added its own publishing house in 1898,
arranged the following year for the education of missionaries
to Africa, pledged support in 1907 for a campaign to end segregation on passenger trains, and steadily worked for the better-
ment of the American black. "Our race and people in America,"
said Morris in 1900, "are like the unwary waters of the mighty
deep — impatient, irrepressible, and determined upon the
amelioration of their condition." Morris, son of Georgia slaves,
was an effective pastor in Helena, Arkansas, when he was chosen
as the NBC's first president. Continuing his pastoral duties
throughout his twenty-eight-year administrative role, he also
combined his commitment to Christian piety with his dedication
to racial integrity. Addressing the National Baptists meeting
in Boston in 1897, Morris lauded his "nation of people . . . made separate in a country for which we have done
more, to the man, to build up than any other people in it . . . ."
Blacks had not sought the separation; as Christians they had
not wanted schism. But now that it had come, perhaps it was
just as well. For in Morris's mind it was clear that "the possibilities of the race, and especially that part represented by the
colored Baptists, would not have been drawn out and made manifest as they have." Creation of a new and separate church has

revealed, as only it could, "a host of intelligent, self-reliant, practical leaders among us . . ."

Schism, however, often turns in upon itself; dissidents find further division easy. Morris in his long tenure of office encountered among the host of intelligent and self-reliant leaders men who grew restless under the authority of the NBC. As blacks had separated from whites in a dispute over publication, now blacks differed with blacks in this same area. The National Baptist Publishing Board, chartered in 1898, was the creation of the National Baptist Convention formed in 1895 — or was it? Publishing board members argued that theirs was a "purely private business institution." By 1915 it was admittedly also a successful one. That success, the board's dynamic founder and leading spirit R. H. Boyd contended, is the result of "many years of labor and hardship" on the part of the board members themselves, labor "not only to promote the interest of the denomination, but to demonstrate to the world what our people could do for themselves in this particular way." Not so, said the authorities of the NBC. The publishing board had succeeded only because it had the "donation, patronage, and moral support of the churches, district association and state conventions making up the National Baptist Convention." Could this division be healed so that black Baptists in America might remain a powerful united force?

The answer, unfortunately, was no. The position of the NBC was weakened by the fact that, not being legally incorporated, it could not hold title to property in its own name. In 1915 the NBC remedied the situation by becoming a legal entity, but the lock had come too late to the barn door. The publishing board, maintaining its own independence financially, proceeded to declare its independence ecclesiastically by creating another National Baptist Convention, this one proudly and disdainfully "Unincorporated." The original body, "without a pencil or a mailing list," was obliged to create afresh another agency for the publication and distribution of its own literature. It did so, and both bodies — the original National Baptist Convention, Incorporated, and the derivative National Baptist Convention, Unincorporated — pressed on with vigor. Both bodies, moreover, continued to testify to that "pride of race" that found expression and opportunity in separate ecclesiastical organizations. Schism for the sake of race was the response of those black American Christians who had felt, and were still to feel, a sorrow, disappointment, and resentment that reverberated through even the most hallowed halls.

Ecumenism

Bringing churches together also drives them apart. The ecumenical movement's strangest irony is that whenever the choir joyfully sings of "The Church's One Foundation," at that moment a few new cracks appear in those foundations. Every merger calls for some flexibility, some compromise, some fresh perception of what is essential and what peripheral. If votes are taken, rarely are they unanimous. If new creeds are adopted, rarely is this accomplished without giving offense to some. In the very act of binding up, healing, conciliating, and loving — even there schism is born.

Such schisms, though regularly noisy, are often tiny. Most church mergers are consummated only after the most arduous, patient, and protracted courtship — a courtship of such complex choreography as to bewilder the outsider. Even with advance briefing and detailing program notes, the observer can rarely detect the magic moment when the path suddenly turns smooth or the fatal step that causes everything to fall apart. An assembly that one year is filled with optimism is the next year heavy with gloom, and explanations for the sharp shift fail to convince. Awkward ecclesiastical machinery together with tedious verbosity suggest that denominational marriages must be made in heaven, if at all. On the other hand, the very complexity, the extended tedium, prevent mergers from being precipitate and offer to the dissident or dubious their full days in court. Normally, then, only a small minority finds it necessary to set out on that long, lonesome road of schism.

In twentieth-century America, few church mergers* have totally escaped this "splinter effect." More surprising, perhaps, is that the splinters have generally been so short-lived. Mere resistance to an ecclesiastical marriage, whether from fidelity to history or liturgy, to polity or theology, has not constituted sufficient thrust for a burgeoning new church. The resistance has, nonetheless, been strong and strident at the time of merger; schism is elaborately defended and the "ecumaniacs" scornfully denounced.

In 1957 the Congregational Christian churches joined with the Evangelical and Reformed churches to create the United Church of Christ. That simple sentence serves up a sizeable slice of ecumenical history. In 1931 New England's Congregationalists absorbed remnants of the O'Kelly schism* and other frontier "Christians." In 1934, the Evangelical and Reformed church came into being when two groups of German pietists united on the basis of their common cultural heritage. Only two decades after these ecclesiastical marriages, additional proposals for organic church unity were made. German pietists, frontier egalitarians, Puritan progeny: how much did these three groups

---

*The mergers in this century include the following: Northern Baptist Convention and Free Baptist churches (1911); three Norwegian Lutheran synods (1917); Presbyterians and Welsh Calvinist Methodists (1920); Dutch Reformed and Hungarian Reformed (1924); Congregational and Christian churches (1931); German Evangelical and German Reformed (1934); northern and southern branches of Methodism (1939); northern and Scottish Presbyterians (1958); the Unitarians and the Universalists (1961); the formation of the American Lutheran church in 1960 followed two years later by the creation of the Lutheran Church in America. The decade of the 1960s also witnessed the extensive deliberations of the Consultation of Church Union (COCU), an ambitious effort to unite ten denominations within American Protestantism: northern and southern Presbyterians, the Methodist church together with three predominantly black Methodist groups, the Episcopal church, the Disciples of Christ, the United Church of Christ (formerly Congregationalists), and the Evangelical United Brethren. The last named group united with the Methodists in 1968; in 1972 the northern Presbyterians withdrew from the Consultation on Church Union.

*See above, p. 13f.

have in common? How fruitful or reasonable or peaceful would their union be? In the light of history, theology, and contemporary Christianity, what justification existed for the 1957 merger?

Organized opposition to that merger came chiefly from those of Congregational heritage. The very name "congregational" provided one basis for resistance. As a description of church government, "congregational" implied not an ever-enlarging denominational bureaucracy but a continued cherishing of the local churches' right to self-rule. Fellowship among the churches was acceptable, rule over the churches was not. That argument had roots that went deep into history, reaching royal prerogatives and episcopal persecutions, religious wars and social strains, exile and new colonies in a New World. While all these dimensions of ecclesiastical authority were not present in the 1950s, the issue still had plenty of life: freedom versus coercion, isolation versus cooperation, individualism versus the company store, and a simple rural America versus an intricate urban America.

Within Congregationalism's ranks, the lines were clearly if unevenly drawn. Douglas Horton, the denomination's chief executive officer from 1938 to 1956, distinguished two understandings of how churches work together. The first, which he called Congregationalism A, sees all denominational organs and agencies as directly responsible to and controlled by the local church membership. According to this perception, the whole national fellowship "could be no more adventurous than the most conservative of its local churches." Congregationalism B, in contrast, sees a national agency as controlled by its own members who "are in fellowship with the local churches." According to the latter model, the national communion "does not need to delay advance until all its parts are ready." Type A impedes progress, is anachronistic and ill-suited to any change, while Type B offers the kind of tactical flexibility necessary "to outguess and out-maneuver anti-Christian forces which are organized at higher levels than that of the village or local district." With his own preference never in doubt, Horton warned that "the rocks are full of fossils of species not flexible enough to change with the changing times and grow with the growing world; but I do not believe that the Congregational Christian Churches are destined to be bed-fellows to Brontosaurus."

Brontosaurus or not, Congregationalism A had its sturdy defenders. In 1955, the National Association of Congregational Christian Churches was formed in Detroit, Michigan. Representing at least one hundred local churches, the association pointed with alarm to the dangers of merger: local churches would lose their voice and perhaps even their property, would be drawn into a "strange" denomination whose theological and ecclesiastical character was quite unknown, would helplessly stand by as their own members were shorn of freedoms for which ancestors had died. The Reverend Malcolm K. Burton, leading anti-merger spokesman, saw the entire ecumenical thrust as a deceptively dangerous one. The average church member thinks merger a good thing for it must mean a liquidation of many "denominational overhead organizations which so often try to dominate the local churches." Regrettably, it does not work that way. While the laity is thinking of liquidation, the "ecumenical leaders are thinking of pyramiding those ecclesiastical organizations, and of making the local churches count for even less than they do today." Resistance to bureaucracy is closer to the spirit of Jesus than is the embracing of some megachurch. Opponents of the merger should not be characterized as selfish or stubborn or isolationist; they merely seek freedom in the name of the Gospel, convinced that "only such freedom can be true to the nature of the Master."

As deliberations continued and as preliminary votes were taken, the divergence between "A" and "B" widened. The National Association was joined by such other groups as the Committee for the Continuation of the Congregational Christian Churches and the League to Uphold Congregational Principles. These anti-merger forces argued that tradition must be honored,

not subverted; ignoring a great heritage hardly constitutes loyalty
to it. Furthermore, if anyone was talking "schism" it must be
the proponents of the merger. For, by pushing this shot-gun
marriage upon unwilling partners, they will end up with more
denominations than they had in the beginning. Two denominations will not become one, but will create three or even four.
Since a forced unity will only bring further division, the true
ecumenists are those who resist the merger! It was an ingenious
argument — preserve unity by opposing union — and it might
have worked had the contrary forces been more evenly divided.

Despite all dire predictions and all energetic efforts, the forces
opposing the merger remained small. When the Congregationalists joined with the Evangelical and Reformed in 1957,
Plymouth Rock did not split in two. Only a modest-sized chip
was knocked away at the uniting synod held in Cleveland, Ohio.
Enemies of the merger argued that "1,400,000 Congregationalists in 5,549 free churches" could never be induced to join that
"phantom creation," the United Church of Christ. The vast
majority, however, were so induced, while the one hundred
churches of the national association grew to only about three
hundred a decade after the marriage was complete. Friends of
the merger saw the creation of the United Church as a "witness
to the reconciling, healing, emancipating power of God's love."
In this one act American Protestantism, they exclaimed, had
"turned away from division toward union, from individualism
toward cooperation, from preoccupation with secondary matters
to concern for the central evangelical mission of the church."
At the nuptial feasting, let there be dancing and much joy.
For the schismatics, however, the wine was sour and the joy
was gone. The way of schism is hard.

A nation still young was with respect to schism already old.*

---

*As yet, one cannot write of schism whose primary justification is sexist discrimination.
The continued resistance of several major denominations, however, to a full and equal
ministry for women suggests that such a chapter may soon be written.

The pain, the promise, the delusion, the delight — all were there, in uneven amounts, in every schism. Sinning against love was a rough, tortuous, uncertain road; yet, many of America's restless religious flock chose to take it. Whether the road eventually led to the Celestial Kingdom, only the patient, persisting pilgrim knew.

3

The Heretics: Sinners Against Faith

Without an established church, schism in America is where one defines it. Without an official orthodoxy, heresy must also be in the stipulations of the definer. However defined, heresy easily slips from the pursuer's grasp, this not only because of the heretic's cautious ambiguity but because of the believer's over-eager conciliation and concession. In America one has to work hard to maintain an heretical status. At least since the colonial period, the infidel, as Martin E. Marty has noted, "had to fight to be infidel, to avoid being absorbed by the vague, protean outreaches of evangelicalism."

The problem of definition was less severe in G. K. Chesterton's England, though even there Anglicanism and Catholicism were not in full theological agreement. In 1905 Chesterton published his *Heretics*, following that book three years later with the "positive side," namely, *Orthodoxy*. In his relaxed, witty, modish apologia for Roman Catholicism, Chesterton was not so much seeking to define heresy as to get rid of it. Western man, even in the first decade of the twentieth century, was less fixed in his cosmic position, less assured in his religious declarations. Against modern man's bemused and cavalier attitude toward theological opinion, Chesterton asserted that "the most practical and important thing about a man is still his view of the universe." Not only the most practical, it is also the most human. "Man can be defined as an animal that makes dogmas." Civilization emerges not because of man's ability as tool-maker or as food-gatherer but because of his genius for firmly held ideas. Trees, on the other hand, "have no dogmas. Turnips are singularly broad-minded." To be sure, burning a man at the stake for his ideas is both absurd and impractical; only one thing is more absurd and impractical, "the habit of saying that his philosophy does not matter."

The modern world has an understandable skittishness about taking a man's ideas, his philosophy, too seriously. So much bigotry and fanaticism has inspired so much persecution and torture for "mere opinion" that the desire for a repeat performance is, one assumes, largely gone. But ideas do have consequences, as even the most pragmatic among us admit. Ideas of genetic inferiority, of doctrinal superiority, of political loyalty, of historic inevitability, of ethical responsibility — these ideas have had consequences of terrifying proportion in the history of man. If the suppression of ideas is evil and self-defeating, the flippant dismissal of ideas as irrelevant to the world's business is reckless and self-deluding. It is a measure of the worth of history's heretics that they have affirmed in their lives, and often in their deaths, that ideas do matter.

But who are America's heretics? Certainly not the mindless wonders of a superficial secularity for whom the territory of religious opinion is as uninteresting as it is unknown. Certainly not the tender souls trapped in parochial sectarian strife about liberalism and conservatism, about symbolic and literal truth, about biblical understandings and creedal modifications. The latter may even find themselves caught in heresy trials, but such trials do not represent the real heterodoxy in America, only a disagreement about the precise boundaries of orthodoxy. Full-blooded heresies hardly know the boundaries are there, or if they know they do not care.

If one searches for a plumb line of "orthodoxy" in America, the ancient Judeo-Christian heritage of an ethical, personal monotheism may be as close as one can come. The symphony

of religion in America contains many phrases and subtle
melodies, but the dominant theme historically and liturgically
is this: "Hear, O Israel, the Lord thy God is one God . . ."
The God of the Shema and of the early creeds, a powerful and
providential Being from whom all blessings flow, is a God over
history, in history, and at the end of history. To dissent from
that "view of the universe" is to worship no longer at the major
shrines of America; it is to withdraw from the religion of the
Republic; it is to sin against faith. The heretics whom we shall
consider all stand at one point in their lives within that Judeo-
Christian world view. They have, however, scrutinized that view
closely only to find it in one or more respects sadly deficient:
repressive or irrational, insensitive or warped, obscurantist or
confused, mean-spirited or simply wrong.

A Reasonable World

Historians have long noted the flowering of genius that graced
the early years of the American Republic. Men of learning, of
curiosity, of imagination, of energy, and of hope were the real
promise of that New Age they foresaw. Equally remarkable was
the degree of consensus among these philosopher-kings, these
enlightened revolutionaries. In that famous introductory phrase,
"We hold these truths to be self-evident . . . , " the impressive word is "we." Truths commonly held, collectively affirmed,
in unity fought for and won. One of the truths shared in the
Revolutionary era was that the religion pervading the Western
world suffered serious inadequacies. Institutional religion was
folly, to be sure, but the criticism was deeper than that, touching
the foundation of all doctrine. Any world view that based itself
upon a divine revelation was an irrational world view. Mankind
has only one revelation — his capacity to reason. Reason is the
arbiter of all truth, reason is the voice of God to man. And
men of reason must dethrone or destroy the hoary idols of the
mind.

Even the nineteen-year-old Benjamin Franklin (1706–1790) found no need for revelation or ecclesiastical tradition as he undertook to describe "the general State of Things in the Universe." In *A Dissertation on Liberty and Necessity*, published in 1725 in a carefully limited edition, Franklin mocked the received views regarding virtue and vice, compulsion and freedom, pleasure and pain. Indeed, in his youthful skepticism he virtually mocked reason itself. For his tightly logical little essay ended up proving the existence of a world that few would care to live in. With that kind of tongue-in-cheekiness in which a mature Franklin reveled, the bold youth calmly explained that his argument could do no harm; for it, like everything else in the universe, must be good and wise since all that exists is at the pleasure of a good, wise, almighty God. "The Order and Course of Things will not be affected by Reasoning of this kind . . ." An older Franklin, less skeptical or at least more prudent, regarded the writing of this brief tract as one of the "errata" of his life.

America had much more sustained and determined heretics for reason's sake in the persons of Ethan Allen, Elihu Palmer, and above all Thomas Paine. Allen (1737–1789), Vermont's Revolutionary hero, in 1784 published, with some difficulty, *Reason the Only Oracle of Man, Or, A Compenduous System of Natural Religion. Alternately adorned with Confutations of a Variety of Doctrines incompatible to it; Deduced from the most exalted Ideas which we are able to form of the Divine and Human Characters, and from the Universe in General.* Drawing heavily on the ideas and notes of his collaborator, Thomas Young (a medical itinerant who died before the work was finished), Allen like Franklin dismisses the God of Christian revelation. A God known chiefly for his miracles and his penchant for eternal punishment is not worthy of worship. Mistaken notions regarding divine inspiration or revelation, furthermore, have done more "to delude mankind in religious matters" than any other thing. Unlike Franklin, however, Allen did not see the distinctions between good and evil as erased

or man's freedom swallowed up in some all-consuming cosmic
Necessity. On the contrary, the providence of God does not
in any way interfere with the free choices of man, "for God
cannot control the actions of free beings, since, if he did, it
would be a contradiction to their being free." Even Omnipotence
itself cannot create a contradiction. Since necessity and freedom
are "diametrically opposed to each other," then "we cannot in
truth be said to act necessarily and freely in the same action."
There is, of course, nothing intrinsically heretical in this classic
argument. Allen's heresy lies in his rejection of all insight into
that problem that does not come in the name of reason, mankind's only standard. When reason brings its judgments to bear
upon revelation, the latter is seen to be "either originally a deception" or else it has since "by adulterations become spurious."
Reason is not one of many avenues, not one among many well-
springs of truth: it is man's only oracle.

So it was also for Elihu Palmer (1764–1806), graduate of
Dartmouth ('87) and member of the still infant, still secret society of Phi Beta Kappa. Blinded by an attack of yellow fever
in 1793, Palmer gave all his energies and passion for the cause
of reason, against the cause of religion. His major work, *Principles
of Nature*, published in 1802, exalted Reason as "the glory of
our nature"; Reason was destined "to overturn the empire of
superstition and erect upon its ruins a fabric against which the
storms of despotism may beat in vain." Plainly, the despotism
he had in mind was religion. Theological systems, claiming to
be of divine origin, are "among the destructive causes by which
the life of man has been afflicted." That "awful doctrine" of
the Trinity "violates all the rules of arithmetical calculation and
mathematical proportion" even as it "violates all ideas of common
sense and common understanding." The Bible from beginning
to end is but "a vast variety of fact, fable, principle, wickedness
and error." Such is its indecency that one has good ground for
believing the Bible to be "the production of weak and vicious
men, and not the work of infinite wisdom."

The founders of the Western world's great religions, Moses, Jesus, and Muhammad, have as little claim to moral merit "as any three men on the face of the earth."

They were all of them imposters — two of them notorious murderers in practice, and the other a murderer in principle; and their existence united has, perhaps, cost the human race more blood and produced more substantial misery than all the other fanatics of the world.

The presence of a single "perhaps" hardly softens the fury of Palmer's attack upon a religious tradition that was not merely wrong but was criminally insane. If one considers, wrote the angry deist, the kind of a God that Jews and Christians are expected to worship, it would be better for them, and for all mankind, if they had been "destitute of all theological opinions." If, on the other hand, men will turn from superstition to truth, from revelation to science and virtue, then man will be what Nature intended him to be: "a standing evidence of the divinity of thought and the unlimited power of human reason." Heretical rationalism had no more devoted advocate.

It did have, however, a more powerfully persuasive one: Thomas Paine (1737–1809). If Ethan Allen's influence was limited by a fire that destroyed most of the copies of his dangerous book, if Elihu Palmer was circumscribed by a difficult personality and a physical disability, and if Franklin took pains to keep his "erratum" from being too widely known, Paine suffered no such liabilities. Enormously popular during and just after the American Revolution, Thomas Paine moved on to "lead" the revolution in France and — he hoped — in England. During his years in Paris, before his return to America in 1802, Paine wrote *The Age of Reason* (1794, 1796). If that two-volume work was not everywhere read, it was everywhere at least excoriated and condemned. The indiscretions of a youthful Franklin could, if known, be majestically forgiven; the broad barrage of an Allen or a Palmer could be stoically ignored. But the patriot Paine of *Common Sense* and *Crisis Papers*, writing in his full maturity

and in the glow of international notoriety, could not be quietly
shelved. Was Paine really speaking for an entire age, as the
title of his book suggested, or only for the fleeting moment?

Each religion, each church, noted Paine, accuses the other
of unbelief. He will treat each of them with impartial respect:
"I disbelieve them all." Though he regards all with an equal
disdain, his special target clearly is the Judeo-Christian fraud.
For this tradition, based upon the mockeries, obscenities, fables,
and contradictions of biblical "revelation," is the most successful
enslaver of men's minds. The fundamental error of Judaism and
of Christianity, the costly tragic mistake from which all distor-
tion and perversion ooze, is the notion that God reveals himself
in a written word that is authoritative for all mankind. That
idea is the purest nonsense. Consider the fact that the Bible
is written in the language of men. Such language is "local and
changeable"; such language, moreover, is an excellent vehicle
for counterfeiting and lying; and when such language is subject
to the vagaries of translation, it is a regular means for "mistaking
the sense" altogether. God has only one universal language: the
creation of the world. In this word and this word only "God
speaketh universally to man." Only in listening to this word
is mankind neither duped nor deceived.

If the very notion of a written revelation is absurd, that absur-
dity is many times confounded by the particular "revelation"
known as the Old and the New Testaments. Much of Paine's
first volume and virtually all of his second, published two years
later, is a direct, unrelenting attack upon biblical material. Not
particularly profound, the attack is sweeping, uncompromising,
devastating. Paine's own figure is an apt one: "I have now gone
through the Bible as a man would go through a wood with
an axe on his shoulder and fell trees."

If revelation has any meaning at all, Paine argues, it must
be a communication of something not known before. "For if I
have done a thing, or seen it done, it needs no revelation to
tell me I have done it, or seen it . . ." Now, much of what

one reads in the Bible is simply anecdote or narrative and has, therefore, nothing whatever to do with revelation.

> When Samson ran off with the gate-posts of Gaza, if he ever did so (and whether he did or not is nothing to us), or when he visited his Delilah, or caught his foxes, or did anything else, what has revelation to do with these things? If they were facts, he could tell them himself . . . and if they were fictions, revelation could not make them true; and whether true or not, we are neither the better nor the wiser for knowing them.

So much for the Bible as revelation on logical grounds. On ethical grounds, the judgment is even more harsh.

> Whenever we read the obscene stories, the voluptuous debaucheries, the cruel and torturous executions, the unrelenting vindictiveness, with which more than half the Bible is filled, it would be more consistent that we called it the word of a demon than the Word of God. It is a history of wickedness that has served to corrupt and brutalize mankind; and, for my own part, I sincerely detest it, as I detest everything that is cruel.

For Paine the conclusion is inescapable: all the miseries of man, all the bloody wars and persecutions of European history, all the cruelty and lusts have their origin in a single, sad delusion: "this impious thing called revealed religion . . . this monstrous belief that God has spoken to man." The "pretended thing" that we call revealed religion has taught "nothing that is useful to man and everything that is dishonorable to his Maker." Revelation's final catastrophe is that it causes man to give up all notion of virtue, all sense of principle, all discrimination between fable and fact. "A man, by hearing all this nonsense lumped and preached together, confounds the God of the Creation with the imagined God of the Christians, and lives as if there were none."

The Age of Reason was a damning indictment, unrelieved by any ambiguity, untempered by any disposition to see "the other side." When soon after its publication the French nation was ripped apart, the Church in France disgraced, and Reason herself

enthroned it was terrifyingly clear that the price of heresy runs
high. Determined that such a price not be exacted in America,
the apostles of orthodoxy and the enemies of deism launched
a powerful and ultimately successful counteroffensive. Attacked
by the likes of Allen, Palmer, and Paine, orthodoxy's generals
called not for retreat but advance. Bible societies sprang up in
abundance, missionaries in great numbers were sent not only
to the American West but to Hawaii and around the world.
Pious seminaries were built and pastoral letters issued warnings
against the "exterminating infidels." A Second Great Awakening
saved a young and vulnerable nation from infidelity, from mortal
folly and immortal damnation. Heresy had fallen; orthodoxy was
secure. Or, was heresy only being purveyed in subtler, smoother
forms?

A Romantic World

Romanticists fell in love with everything — except orthodoxy.
Persons with so all-encompassing an embrace do not easily
become heretics; indeed, from the standpoint of "religion in
general," the romanticists were allies, not enemies. They stood
against the hard-line rationalism of an Ethan Allen or the
thoroughgoing materialism of a Thomas Hobbes, protesting the
reductionism of man's religious dimension. Man does have a
spiritual nature; so does the Universe. God can be known as
immediately and as certainly — in truth, more so — as all the
facts of Bacon's science, as all the data of Gibbon's history. No,
the romanticists are not the most obvious choice for heresy's
hall of fame.

Only as they fend off rigid dogmatisms and slough off threadbare creeds does a hint of heresy float by, like a tiny innocent
cloud. Notwithstanding that fluffy innocence, romanticism could
make orthodoxy just as uneasy, defensive, and hostile as rationalism did. In New England where all currents ran strong, the
mutual animosity of rationalism, romanticism, and orthodoxy

is amply documented. There, as Perry Miller noted, "theological disputation and fine logical distinguishing had long been a major industry." Under rationalism's banner, Unitarianism had broken Calvinism's monopolistic hold upon the New England mind. Now under romanticism's banner (along with others), transcendentalism concluded that the new rigidity of Unitarianism was no more palatable than the old orthodoxy of Cambridge synods and Saybrook platforms. Some Unitarians, in turn, found the heresy of this new romanticism, the "party of the Future," more horrifying, more personally insulting, than even the Calvinist theologians did. Andrews Norton, professor in the Unitarian-dominated Harvard Divinity School, spoke for his fellows when he described transcendentalism as "the latest form of infidelity." It seemed to say so much about religious feeling, so little about religious fact. These latter-day infidels reject historical Christianity, reject revelation, reject miracles, reject the analysis and the investigation and the testimony of the scholarly authorities. Their religion, said Norton, "exists merely, if it exists at all, in undefined and unintelligible feelings. . . . " Transcendentalists are not satisfied with the probabilities that scientific investigation brings forth: they want intuitive certainties! " . . . the solid earth is not stable enough for them to rest on. They have firm footing on the clouds." Another of Harvard's Unitarian professors, Francis Bowen, summed up neatly the contest between his co-religionists and the transcendentalists: "Either one party or the other is entirely in the wrong. To come over to the new system we must read our former lessons backwards. . . . "

Transcendentalism, filled with vision, verve, and rippling optimism, would agree that man should throw away his old lesson book and get a new one: nature and his own soul. What Emerson called "corpse-cold Unitarianism" needed to be replaced by a direct apprehension of life-giving eternal truths. To assist in elucidating those nourishing truths, transcendentalism drew from many wells: German idealism as mediated by Carlyle and Coleridge; Oriental philosophy, especially as contained in the

Upanishads; and mystical piety, for which early New England
itself was the source. With this remarkable blend, the romanticists would offer spiritual succor to a generation, and to future
generations. For man does not live by bread, or even by creed,
alone. The blood must warm, the heart must race, the spirit
must lift. And if orthodoxy cannot bring a fresh flush to life,
then heresy must.

Orestes Brownson (1803–1876) made a fascinating if winding
pilgrimage from a youthful hardcore Calvinism to a mature and
aggressive Roman Catholicism, touching along the way nearly
every trend or tenet of nineteenth-century religion in America.
Transcendentalism constituted one of his way stations. Moving
to Massachusetts in 1834, Brownson quickly joined in the intellectual ferment and lively conversation always symbolized by
and often centered in the Transcendental Club. That informal
group, meeting four or five times a year in Boston or Concord
or Chelsea or elsewhere nearby, had its beginning in 1836. For
nearly a decade Brownson expounded and defended the unsettling
principles of New England's newest heresy. A negative and lifeless Unitarianism no longer satisfies; an outmoded and irrelevant
orthodoxy no longer nourishes. Men, weary of doubt and division, cry out "from the bottom of their hearts for faith, for
love, for union." The sickness is not America's alone; all of
Western civilization has found religion to be "but an empty
name" and society generally a valley of dry bones. In Western
Europe no less than in the United States, the sick at heart are
seeking "some crumbs of the bread of life to keep them from
starving."

Brownson hoped to provide a few crumbs in 1836 when he
published a small book entitled, *New Views of Christianity, Society,
the Church*. Christianity in nineteenth-century America, he
wrote, bears little resemblance to its first-century model. Then
it was a sovereign, now it is a shadow; then it commanded both
obedience and respect, now it commands neither; then it had
breathed into it a living soul, only the body now remains. The

church has lost its capacity to communicate vital spiritual truth so that we must find within ourselves that which none other can give or teach. The history of Christianity is chiefly a history of error and corruption, but fortunately God "gave his richest gift when he gave the capacity for progress." And "progress" becomes a key word for these dissenters, often joined with another favorite, "union." Union means reconciliation, atonement, an acknowledgment at the deepest level that "mankind are my brothers." We understand the unity of men when we realize that "not in Jesus alone does the divine ideal incarnate itself, but in every man, in all men, and that all men are brethren, and possessors of a divine nature."

For three hundred years the church has been on the side of the past, while "the future has been with statesmen and philosophers." The latter have taught the church what the church all this time should have been teaching them: namely, the doctrine of equality (that is, all men are sons of God), and the doctrine of progress (that is, man is perfectible in both the spiritual and the material realms). However tardily the church has come to a perception of these basic truths, Brownson adds, she must now begin to proclaim them boldly. If the church fails once more, then "a new temple will arise." For religion does have the power to transform the world in which we live. We have had enough of analysis, negation and dissection: the time to act has come. "He who would have faith must go forth and act."

All orthodoxies are bankrupt, all sects are intellectual vacuums, all ministrations of contemporary Christianity are timid or pointless or pernicious. Brownson found hope in the temple of transcendentalism, but he — as the very embodiment of dissent — discovered this temple to be an inadequate shrine. Ever the restless pilgrim, Brownson was too much a maverick to be only Emerson's echo or a passive scribe for Bronson Alcott's "Orphic" thoughts. For a time he shared the sentiments and the company of New England's apostates from Calvinism and

Unitarianism; in 1844 he became transcendentalism's most
notorious apostate when he entered Boston's one Roman Catholic
church. Heresy, like schism, develops a momentum of its own.

He left behind him, however, a still bubbling intellectual
ferment. Among such men as Emerson, Thoreau, Alcott, Theodore Parker, George Ripley, James Freeman Clarke, William
Henry Channing, and others, one woman fully shared the excite-
ments of the inner circle: Margaret Fuller (1810–1850). Pos-
sessed of remarkable intellectual and physical energies, despite
nagging ill-health, Margaret Fuller compressed the biblically
allotted three-score years and ten into her brief span of forty
years. At the age of twenty-five, assuming heavy family obligations, she began teaching in Bronson Alcott's Temple School
in Boston and offered private lessons in German and Italian.
After two years' teaching in Providence, Rhode Island (1837–
39), she returned to Boston to edit *The Dial*, transcendentalism's principal literary organ.* She wrote poems, published
translations from the German, held famous "conversations" for
Boston ladies, traveled to the American West, joined Horace
Greeley's *New York Tribune* in 1844, published *Woman in the
Nineteenth Century* the following year, visited England, Scotland,
and France in 1846, shared Italy's revolutionary spirit in 1847
and 1848, married an Italian nobleman and had a child, sailed
for America in 1850, and was with her new family lost in ship-
wreck near home.

In the midst of all this, Margaret Fuller became so central
a part of the Transcendental Club that, following her death,
Emerson, Clarke, and W. H. Channing published her *Memoirs*,
adding their reminiscences and tributes. Margaret Fuller's search

*"A Magazine for Literature, Philosophy and Religion," *The Dial* set forth its purpose
in language that indicates how transcendentalism could attract and hold such diverse
elements: "The pages of this Journal will be filled by contributors, who possess little
in common but the love of intellectual freedom, and the hope of social progress; who
are united by sympathy of spirit, not by agreement in speculation; whose faith is in
Divine Providence, rather then in human prescription; whose hearts are more in the
future than in the past; and who trust the living soul rather then the dead letter."

for oneness in the Universe led her, as it did other romantics, along the path of mysticism. While she had her mystical moments, she did not, in Emerson's opinion, ever reach that "absolute or prophetic mount." Yet, her frequent approaches to that spiritual ecstasy, her avid interest in the "literature of asceticism and rapturous piety," gave "a religious dignity to her thought." Clarke noted her drive to develop fully her whole nature, to have "a full experience of life," adding that this passion of hers was "wholly religious, almost Christian." It was religious because of the intensity of her aspiration and the assurance of her vision of human perfectability. Almost Christian but not quite, because Margaret Fuller, said Clarke, had an impatient disdain for the plodding pedestrianism of humanity's common herd. And Channing saw in Margaret Fuller a devotion to the Newness called transcendentalism that was inspiring; she led the way in that "pilgrimage from the idolatrous world of creeds and rituals to the temple of the Living God in the Soul." She silenced "tradition and formulas that the Sacred Oracle might be heard through intuitions of the single-eyed and pure-hearted."

So spoke her friends on her behalf. On her own behalf, Margaret Fuller did not write extensively on the subject of religion. An exciting conversationalist and demanding literary critic, she let through only scattered rays of her special illumination. Clearest of all was her steely determination not to be taken in, not to be duped by orthodoxy's soporific assurances. "I wish to know and to feel my pain, to investigate its nature and its source." A time will come, she conceded, when "the ardors of Search and Action" are too much, a time when she will choose "to lean on something above." But that time is not anticipated as some sweet refuge or comfortable haven; in fact, "the thought of that calmer era is to me a thought of deepest sadness." Like other transcendentalists she found the rupture from orthodoxy in some ways painful and difficult; nevertheless, to remain in that womb any longer was insufferable agony and spiritual death. "I am yet ignorant of the religion of Revelation," but of the

religion of "Beauty and Perfection" there is no doubt: one's heart
affirms it. It is the heart that makes possible whatever faith
man can muster. Not Ethan Allen's reason, that low, limited,
merely technical faculty of the mind. On the command of Jesus
to "Have faith in God," Margaret Fuller meditates as follows:

> O, Direction most difficult to follow! O, counsel most mighty of im-
> port! . . . Yes, this is indeed the beginning and the end of all
> knowledge and virtue; the way and the goal; the enigma and its solu-
> tion. The soul cannot prove to herself the existence of a God; she can-
> not prove her own immortality; she cannot prove the beauty of virtue,
> or the deformity of vice; her own consciousness, the first ground of
> this belief, cannot be compassed by the reason, that inferior faculty
> which the Deity gave for practical, temporal purposes only. This con-
> sciousness is divine; it is part of the Deity; through this alone we
> sympathize with the imperishable, the infinite, the nature of things.

Both Orestes Brownson and Margaret Fuller stood on the edge
of the effort to reshape New England's prevailing orthodoxy.
Both were too deeply involved in their own "Eternal Progression"
to give full attention to New England's evolution. And both
played out their lives on a wider stage than even Boston provided.
Theodore Parker (1810–1860) stands at the center of the New
England drama — guiding, reproving, inspiring, doing whatever needed to be done to usher in a New Age. He was, said
his good friend James Freeman Clarke, Boston's Socrates but
also Boston's John the Baptist, "the prophet of a transition state,
when the law had ended, but the gospel only just begun." A
graduate of Harvard Divinity School in 1836, Parker moved
ever farther from creeds, rituals, and biblical "proofs" to truth
granted through the intuitions of the soul. A scholar of omnivor-
ous appetite and phenomenal memory, Parker used reason's most
sophisticated weaponry to argue on behalf of spirit and feeling.
In turning so sharply away from rationalism Parker offended
his Unitarian brethren and earned their unforgiving enmity.
Shunned by his colleagues and denied the larger pulpits, Parker
moved to Boston's Melodeon, then to its Music Hall where three

thousand persons could gather to hear "God's great gift" to New England. Even before that large public forum had been provided, Parker's resolve was firm.

I will study seven or eight months of the year, and four or five months I will go about, and preach and lecture in city and glen, by the road-side and field-side, and wherever men and women can be found. I will go eastward and westward, and southward and northward, and make the land *ring*; and if this New England theology, that cramps the intellect and palsies the soul of us does not come to the ground, then it shall be because it has more truth in it than I have ever found.

None could mistake Parker's intention or his determination. He had a whole region and a whole generation to re-educate. He must show what is real and eternal in religion as opposed to what is fake and temporal. Miracles, revelations, prophets, even history itself — religion rests on none of these. Though they may have much value in themselves and though our lives may be poorer without them, they do not constitute the essence of religion. Men must come to see that religion rests upon unchanging truth, not upon the fashions and forms in which that truth, in any age, happens to be presented. The great truths of Christianity, for example, no more rest upon the authority of Jesus than do "the axioms of geometry rest upon the personal authority of Euclid or Archimedes." Truth does not rest upon authority, but quite the other way around.

The same principle applies to biblical authority and "infallible inspiration." What if this record is found to be crammed with error? (And Parker was among the very first in America to read and absorb the "higher criticism" of German biblical scholar-ship.) Will Christianity then fall? No, it will not, for all the details of the biblical account form the "foundation of a theology, not of Christianity." This eternal religion does not "stand or fall with the infallible inspiration of a few Jewish fishermen," nor does it survive through "the forebearance of some critic, who can cut when he will the thread upon which its life

depends." If Christianity is true, it needs no other buttress or
authority "as for someone to support Almighty God." Religion,
if true, stands by itself, and Christianity — "that pure
religion"— is always the same, "eternal in the constitution of
the soul and the mind of God."

The perennial problem of orthodoxy, Trinitarian or Unitarian,
Protestant or Catholic, is that it sees Christianity only in terms
of its outer garments. Defenders of orthodoxy see "the removal
of a theological error for the destruction of all religion"; they
believe in the husks of religion and then "condemn others for
not doing the same." All this delusion will depart when men
see that Christianity "is a simple thing . . . absolute, pure,
morality; absolute, pure religion." Its only creed: there is a God;
its only form: "a divine life — doing the best thing in the best
way, from the highest motives." The New Age will have come,
said Parker, when nations ultimately learn that this religion is
the only one there is: "free goodness, free piety, connected with
free thought." When this lesson is finally absorbed, "What a
beautiful world we shall have — what societies of men and of
nations!"

The orthodox will argue that Christianity cannot be stripped
down to these bare bones. Too much of the richness of history
is lost. Too much of the distinctive virtues of a specific tradition
are forsaken. But this is to look at things in a perverse manner,
Parker explains. One has gained freedom and lost nothing; one
has learned how to go forward instead of forever turning backward. By steady stages, we emancipate ourselves from the artifi-
cial, the imperfect, the limited, in order to be restored "to God,
the primeval fountain, whence the church, the Scripture, and
Jesus have drawn all the water of life, wherewith they filled
their urns."

Parker's assault was frontal. From other pulpits as well, the
winds of transcendental doctrine beat steadily upon the house
of nineteenth-century orthodoxy in America. In his early history
of that dissenting movement, O. B. Frothingham observes that

"the church stood fast, because it was allied with power and
fashion, not because it was supported by reason or faith." That
trenchant remark could apply to much of America's religion after
all the gales of New England infidelity had been spent. The
churches did stand, they even grew. New societies and new
measures responded to the challenges of a robust, rapidly expand-
ing Republic. Yet, the pink cheeks betokened fever more than
good health. Not immediately, but generations later, many of
those thriving churches awoke to discover that all the theological
guts were gone.

A Scientific World

Before the Civil War, orthodoxy was berated for paying too
much attention to facts, placing too much emphasis on the data
of history. Universal principles of reason and cosmic heartbeats
were of far greater significance than events in some far away
Syrian outpost all too many centuries ago. After the Civil War,
in contrast, orthodoxy was condemned for having ignored the
facts, for having flaunted the clear testimony of history and of
the senses. Science presented established religion in the Western
world with a powerful new challenge, a challenge that reached
the level of heresy when science became the only path to truth,
when theology, like myth-making, was an inferior stage of
development through which mankind must now pass. Grown-up
men and women no longer need the baubles, the comforts, the
illusions that the theological myth-makers have heretofore been
so eager to provide.

Scientific activity greatly intensified in the postbellum period
and the application of science to the problems of industry,
agriculture, mining, and communication attracted wide attention. The challenge to established religion was, however, far
more than that. Science became the oracle. Its pronouncements
were infallible not by decree but by general assent. Its devotees
revealed an ascetic discipline and single-mindedness that a non-

monastic nation could only view with awe. And its results! Its
results made resistance or carping a costly, losing game. Confronted by this new priesthood that mediated abundant and
wondrous revelations, orthodoxy was by turns baffled or indig-
nant, fawning or hostile, taken in or shut out. The spirit of
the times opposed Tertullian's assertion, "I believe because it
is absurd." More suitable to the age was the affidavit, "I believe
because it is scientific."

With notable achievements in chemistry, photography, teleg-
raphy, physiology, and even history, John William Draper
(1811–1882) early championed the claims of the natural over
the supernatural, the proper prerogatives of science over the
arrogant pretensions of religion. A native of England, Draper
emigrated to America at the age of twenty-one, received his
medical degree from the University of Pennsylvania in 1836,
taught at Hampton-Sydney College in Virginia, then in 1838
joined the scientific faculty of New York University. Despite
his numerous and significant achievements as a scientist, Draper
reached the American public chiefly as an apologist for a unified,
intelligible, altogether natural world.

In 1874, Draper published his immediately popular *History
of the Conflict between Religion and Science.* Noting the "great and
rapidly increasing departure from the public religious faith" evident both in Europe and America, Draper explained that widespread doubt as due to religion's repression of intellectual freedom. But this "intellectual night . . . is passing away; we live
in the daybreak of better things." While all orthodoxy dampens
and discourages intellectual activity, Draper saw Roman Catholic
orthodoxy as the greatest sinner in this regard. Draper, son of
a Methodist minister, explained that he gave Catholicism special
attention "partly because its adherents compose the majority of
Christendom, partly because its demands are the most preten-
tious, and partly because it has commonly sought to enforce these
demands by the civil power." If one brand of orthodoxy draws
most of the fire, it remains true that all brands, all schools

and systems that restrict or oppose scientific investigation, stand condemned. Like the transcendentalists, Draper sees a New Age at hand, a new departure. Unlike the transcendentalists, he sees it ushered in not by romance and mystery but by stern fact and the "irresistible dominion of law."

The sweep of Draper's book, as of his earlier *History of the Intellectual Development of Europe* (1864), is imposing. The cultures of Greece, Persia, Egypt, and Rome are reviewed along with the rise of Christianity and Islam, the teachings of Vedic and Buddhist scripture, and the functions of the medieval synagogue. What one sees in all of this is preeminently conflict: conflict over the nature of the soul, over the manner of creation, over the shape or the age of the earth, over the "reign of law" in the affairs of men no less than in the affairs of the solar system. In elaborating this theme, Draper shows how Christianity from the very beginning set itself upon a collision course with science. The Church early declared herself the "depository and arbiter of knowledge . . . she became a stumbling-block in the intellectual advancement of Europe for more than a thousand years." God had in Scripture "not only a criterion of truth, but had furnished us all that he intended us to know." In the fifth century of the present era, Saint Augustine pushed matters farther along that disastrous course by making the Bible a tyrant over the mind of man.

The example once set, there was no want of followers; the works of the great Greek philosophers were stigmatized as profane; the transcendently glorious achievements of the Museum of Alexandria were hidden from sight by a cloud of ignorance, mysticism, and unintelligible jargon, out of which there too often flashed the destroying lightnings of ecclesiastical vengeance.

Nothing in the millennium that followed mitigates the conflict or credits the Church.

In America one has the opportunity to see what the more positive role of science can be. The scientific age and the American nation were youngsters together. Together, if religion will stay out of the way, they can bring about a glorious time for all mankind. Science has already accomplished much, as a mere glance at the mortality tables of the last two or three centuries will reveal. So much more can be achieved if only modern man does not take any backward steps into "semi-barbarian ignorance and superstition." Our world of 1874 must not surrender to a power that claims divine authority but is in fact "founded in a cloud of mysteries." The greatest disaster would be to surrender to a religion that "sets itself above reason and common sense," proclaims its hatred of the liberty of thought, and arrogates to itself all authority over the conscience of humanity. That world is gone. Let us enter, with confidence, that new world where "mysteries must give place to facts," where religion must give way to science.

Already, Draper argued, the "spirit of the age" is at work undermining the foundations of religion. "It is not given to religions to endure forever. They necessarily undergo transformations. . . ." Of course, Draper was pleased to do all that he could to help along that "spirit of the age." Another helping hand was that of John Wesley Powell (1834–1902). A Civil War veteran who lost an arm in the battle of Shiloh, Powell began his teaching career at Illinois Wesleyan College in Bloomington in 1865. A lover of nature in both his youth and his maturity, Powell's principal interest lay in geology and his principal influence coursed through the United States Geological Survey. In addition to his administrative duties with that federal bureau, Powell explored the American West, defended the cause of conservation, carefully examined the communal life of the Indians, and — somehow — found time to speculate on the roles of science and religion in the development of men and of civilization.

Religion is transformed at the hands of science, Powell acknowledged; however, science "comes to purify not to slay." In that process of purification, science reveals that man is not at the end of his development nor is Western civilization in decline.

Quite the contrary. Man has moved from savagery to barbarism to civilization and he need not stop there. From civilization he can move on to enlightenment, a stage in which the equality of all is recognized as men move beyond mere biological evolution to an "evolution by endeavor." Through active choice, men in the stage of enlightenment can enlarge the happiness of all, can perfect their adaptation to the physical environment. So "the revelation of science is this: Every generation in life is a step in progress to a higher and fuller life; science has discovered *hope*."

If, however, science is to fulfill its promise, error must be swept aside. In the last years of his life, Powell published *Truth and Error, or the Science of Intellection* (1898), the first volume of a projected but never completed three-volume work. Here Powell strikes out at those false concepts, those dangerous illusions, that prevent science from raising civilization to its highest level. Many stand transfixed "in the revelry developed by the hashish of mystery." When they finally taste what has been promised as the "pure water of truth," they find it utterly insipid. Somehow elaborate theological and philosophical systems seem more intoxicating than "the simple truths discovered by science." Mankind, therefore, must now rid itself of that entire legacy conveyed in "the history of ghosts." Savage man had his ghost who dwelled in stones, streams, mountains, and fire. Barbaric man had his: gods of the Olympic pantheon, gods of the upper regions and lower regions, anthropomorphic gods of nature. Civilized man, likewise, has his ghosts, but it is better not to be too specific about those. When it comes to the current orthodoxy, "I purposely remain silent, lest I should antagonize . . . the views of others about religion. . . ."

Powell harbored no animosity toward ghost-ridden modern man, only sympathy. He has simply not yet passed through what has been a necessary stage in the development of man, even as some have not yet forsaken astrology for astronomy. "When I stand before the sacred fire in an Indian village and

listen to the red man's philosophy, no anger stirs my blood.
I love him as one of my kind. He has a philosophy not unlike
that of my forefathers, though widely separated from my own.
. . ." Not anger, but love, for science does not wish to slay.
To say that science is one's vocation is only to declare that one
gives himself to the cause of mankind. This was Powell's drive,
this was Powell's religion. If the historic religions can only come
to see "that true religion is righteous deed," then they are welcome to join in Powell's vocation. All the great prophets have
perceived this truth, Powell wrote, but their followers "con-
tinually relapsed into ceremony, sacrifice and creed as true religion and forgot religion itself." The scientific heretic, not really
wishing to be a heretic, held out some hope that even Christianity
"in the spirit of the Sermon on the Mount" might eventually
become "the religion of the people."

As scientists themselves, Draper and Powell might be accused
of special pleading as they proclaimed science's religious calling.
As a philosopher and editor, Paul Carus (1852–1919) would
not be subject to that charge, though he was the most extravagant
apologist of all. A native of Germany and, like Draper and
Powell, the son of a Protestant clergyman, Carus came to the
United States when he was in his thirties. He affiliated himself
not with a school or university but with a newly founded journal,
the *Open Court*, launched in Chicago in 1887. Under Carus's
editorship, the journal became a publishing house and the publishing house served as a powerful voice for the new scientific age.
Religion and ethics, placed on a solid scientific foundation,
would both be thoroughly reformed. Writing more than fifty
books himself and sponsoring a new philosophical journal, the
Monist, Paul Carus systematized and popularized the sentiments
of such scientists as Draper and Powell.

Religion as science receives from Carus unrestrained hallelujahs
and booming doxologies. We must no longer think of science
as man-made while religion is made of God. Science too is divine;
it is God's revelation to man; it is in fact his prime mode of

communication with his creatures. "Reason is the divine spark
in man's nature, and science, which is a methodological application of man's reason, affords us the ultimate criterion of truth."
Man is made in the image of God to the extent that he manages
to be a rational creature. Science alone gives full reign and
appropriate homage to that divinely rational faculty. If it is too
much to call science supernatural, it is hardly enough to call
it superhuman. Science eliminates human passions and prej-
udices, liberates men from the bonds of sense perceptions, and
with objective clarity reveals the world of order and unchanging
law. Science is man's "Jacob's ladder which at its bottom touches
the world of sense, while its top reaches in to the heaven of
spirit." Mathematics contains more holiness than do all the sanc-
tuaries and all the dogmas.

With science so deified, what role remains for God? God,
that is, the God of science, sustains and supports the moral
order. Belief in God is equivalent to a declaration of obedience
to the moral law. Science cannot, of course, accept the old
orthodoxy that conceives of God as a supernatural Being. The
allegories and similes of traditional religion must be seen for
what they are — more figures of speech than assertions of fact.
We purge the term "God" of its gross and pagan connotations,
seeing in the word "the authority of the moral ought." Once
our understandings are fully clarified, the designation "God"
takes on new dynamism and excitement. True, the path from
the old orthodoxy to the new may lead for a time to atheism,
"but where has any one found any truth worthy of the name
who had not first to pass to it through doubt and had to gain
it" through pain? In any event, it must be clear that science
does not negate the God-idea; science completes and perfects
it.

In the second half of the nineteenth century, Draper, Powell,
and Carus were joined by numbers of fellow Americans confident
of the potency of science, impatient with the impotence and
confusions of "public religion." The "hashish of mystery" should

be allowed to befuddle the minds of men no longer. On Isaiah's celestial throne, high and lifted up, the Lord no longer sat. There, in his place, was Science, the new deity, the new object of veneration and of worship. When Paul Carus sang his doxology, thousands joined in a hymn of praise to Science from whom all blessings flow. If orthodoxy still had the best tunes, her choir stalls were often empty. Sinners against faith, meanwhile, composed marching songs ever bolder and unrestrained.

An Egocentric World

Orthodoxy is protected against self-centeredness by an omniscient, omnipotent Being whose judgments are sure and whose concerns always include the neighbors. Heresy, too, may have its safeguards: the rationalist bows before Universal Reason, the romanticist before a responding Oversoul, the empiricist before the unyielding data of the sensible world. In the name of God, however, one may give his major attention to man — not to all men, but to a particular man, to the self. In this instance, the hounds of heaven turn out to be the hurts of the world; one flees therefrom to find a peace, a contentment, an ease, a heaven that knows no hell. Cosmic evil has no standing, and private evils — disease, poverty, inferior station, malaise — disappear before corrected understandings, positive thoughts and effective appropriations of spiritual power. He who seeks to save his own soul does not lose it; he is told in detail exactly where and how it may be found.

In the late nineteenth and early twentieth centuries, Mary Baker Eddy (1821–1910) is unique chiefly for the degree of her success. For the age in which she lived blossomed with teachings and techniques appropriate to the new anxieties imposed by enlarging industries, crowded cities, and diminished theologies. Water cures, food cures, sun cures, nature cures, and mind cures rushed into a vacuum from which traditional religion had been emptied and that empirical science had not yet filled. To the needs of the age as to her own personal ills and misfortunes, Mrs. Eddy brought her extraordinary skills as a teacher and her genius as an organizer. A native of New Hampshire, the young Mary, of frail constitution, was repeatedly afflicted with illness. Neither the Congregationalism that she adopted in 1838 nor the marriage she contracted in 1843 brought release from anguish, an anguish both mental and physical. After only eighteen months of marriage, George Washington Glover died; their son, and only child, was born three months later. Afflictions continued, all relief proved illusory. A second marriage in 1853, to Dr. Daniel Patterson, marked no turning point, but the association with Phineas P. Quimby beginning in 1862 did. Quimby's efforts to develop a "science of health" were based upon an understanding of the relationship between ill health and false belief, between well-being and genuine understanding. Mrs. Eddy found herself greatly calmed and powerfully strengthened under Quimby's ministrations. When Quimby died in 1866, Mrs. Eddy revised and expanded his teachings about science and health and religion. In Lynn, Massachusetts, in 1875 her book *Science and Health* first appeared and four years later a formal charter inaugurated the Church of Christ (Scientist). Despite serious defections and often bitter controversies, the young movement enjoyed a full ecclesiastical structure with a growing membership by the time of the founder's death in 1910 in Brookline, Massachusetts.*

Christian Science, Mrs. Eddy explained, is "the quintessence of Christianity, that heals disease and sin and destroys death." The healing is not simply science, it is also religion. For one can only conquer disease or mental error with a proper metaphysics. Classical education is insufficient; biblical knowledge alone is inadequate; metaphysical education is essential. Mrs. Eddy personally offered such education, notably in the Massachusetts Metaphysical College established in 1881. To the whole world she offered it in the authoritative book that went

*Mrs. Eddy's third marriage, to Asa Gilbert Eddy (d. 1882), took place in 1877.

through hundreds of editions. The concluding chapter of the
first edition, "Healing the Sick," declared that all suffering is
mental, not physical. Mind controls matter, but does even more:
it "is the fundamental strength of morality, for it gives control
over sin, sickness and death." If the lungs are ulcerated and
decayed, it is the mind that is responsible: "combat the error
and belief of Life in matter with the Truth that Life is Soul
and not sense, and you will form the lungs anew. . . ." Despite
the signals that the body may send, the fact remains — and
must remain uppermost in one's mind — that "disease is a
belief, its origin mental instead of physical. . . ."

Jesus provides the model of proper healing, for he recognized
that only God is real, all else is illusion and error. In treating
the sick, moreover, "he never recommended materia medica,
hygiene, physiology, etc." Properly understood, the ministry
of Jesus and the Bible contain "all our recipes for healing"— but
these must be properly understood. Though not until 1883 did
a "Key to the Scriptures" become a regular part of *Science and
Health*, Mrs. Eddy's own teaching from the beginning provided
the essential clues for a right interpretation of ancient Scripture.
In its original form, the Key consisted only of a glossary setting
forth "the metaphysical interpretations of Bible terms, giving
their spiritual sense, which is also their original meaning." When
the Bible speaks of "death," for example, we must understand
the real meaning, the key, for that word. It is "an illusion,
the life in matter. . . . Any material evidence of death is false,
for it contradicts the spiritual facts of being." Knowledge is
merely that which is perceived through the five senses, or it
is another name for human doctrines and human opinions; its
contrary is Truth, the spiritual understanding that Jesus first
brought to men and that Christian Science now makes plain.

To be sure, the Truth that reality is spiritual rather than
material is not of itself egocentric. The application of that Truth,
however, by Mrs. Eddy and her followers, was consistently for
the amelioration of personal rather than social ills. Mark Twain,

an early caustic critic of Christian Science, deplored the social indifference of the young movement.

> No charities to support. No, nor even to contribute to. One searches in vain the [Christian Science] Trust's advertisements and the utterances of its organs for any suggestion that it spend a penny on orphans, widows, discharged prisoners, hospitals, ragged schools, night missions, city missions, libraries, old people's homes, or any other object that appeals to a human being's purse through his heart.

A more authoritative source is *Science and Health* itself. In its concluding section called "Fruitage," the faithful offer testimonies to the mighty work wrought by the new doctrine. And the great work is the healing of private pains — above and beyond all else, healing: rheumatism, astigmatism, hernia, fibroid tumor, indigestion, cataract, insomnia, gastritis, cancer, consumption, rickets, dropsy, constipation, tonsilitis, "torpid liver," tuberculosis, and addiction to liquor, tobacco, and profanity. This preoccupation with health, Donald Meyer has written, is "a fatal idea, for ultimately discontent is divine. . . ."

In the dreary days of America's great depression, other voices of promise and hope were heard: "There exists an invisible Spiritual Power which man can use to bring himself whatever material things are necessary . . . a great law . . . which can bring to you in person an abundance of peace, happiness and material supply." Frank B. Robinson (1886–1948) offered this and more to those willing to subscribe to his twenty lessons and pay the forty dollars. A former Baptist minister, then vagrant, then Salvation Army soldier, then pharmacist, Robinson in 1929 saw a new light. In this fresh illumination, all that he had learned from the churches, the theological schools, and his private biblical study faded into insignificance. Having made available to others the truth that he himself had seen, Robinson wrote in 1934, "I think I can safely say that I have in my files more evidence of the workings of the Spirit of God in more lives in five short years than any entire denomination can show in the past fifty years."

Establishing his headquarters in Moscow, Idaho, Robinson through direct mailing and newspaper advertising propagated his good tidings. Rather than sinking monies and energies into ecclesiastical organization and church property, Robinson determined to get the message told. Daily, letters of inquiry or acceptance flowed into Moscow and daily lessons of encouragement and promise flowed out. All during the 1930s and 1940s, this mail-order business of religion boomed. Psychiana, as the movement was called, derived all its authority and all its understanding from Frank B. Robinson himself.

The founder and high-priest of Psychiana provided in 1934 an autobiography more homiletic than biographic, more discursive than ordered. The volume testifies chiefly to its author's certitude regarding Psychiana, "the movement of the Spirit of God on the earth." That his new religion is untraditional, novel, nonbiblical — in short, heretical — is to its credit rather than otherwise.

When the Christian Science church first gave its new vision of Truth to the world, this vision was absolutely contrary to the teachings of the orthodox church. Today, we know that millions of people have found comfort and solace and God through the teachings of the Christian Science Church. To whatever extent people find Peace, Happiness, Joy and the other things of God through any religious teaching, then just to that extent is that teaching of God.

Robinson's message, thus authenticated, went out to an anxious, distraught population: "Has it been a hard day? Do you feel tired out? Are you weary of struggling, of fighting against the desolating forces of envy, bitterness, jealousy, and fear? Then study with us for awhile. . . ." The great GOD-LAW that governs all of nature is just as surely in charge of each individual life. If one accepts this cosmic fact, meditates upon it regularly, affirms its power repeatedly, then one can become whatever he wishes to be. "No matter how dull and spiritless things seem to you now, you can reach out to a never-failing fountain of Power. . . ." Many reached out, and testimonies flowed into Moscow's post office from Ohio, New York, Tennessee, California, Virginia, Minnesota, Texas, and seventy countries around the world. The assurances that full satisfaction had been received were essentially the same: Psychiana "has indeed meant more to me than anything that has ever come into my life, thrill after thrill, exceeding joy, strength in weakness, health in sickness, happiness in worry and trouble . . ."

When Robinson died in 1948, some effort was made to keep the lessons moving out and the money moving in, but the inspiration and the authority were gone. Unlike Christian Science, no careful organization had been built, no sacred text had been provided. Nor was there in Psychiana any sense that its grasp of the secrets of the universe belonged alone to that small circle. Besides, by 1948, American society needed little instruction or encouragement in its pursuit of happiness. For many, God had already become a utensil in that pursuit, religion had become magic, and jaded citizens turned from a wounded world to cultivate their private gardens of hedon. Santayana once asked, "And what should be the end of life, if fellowship with the gods is a means only?" Egocentric religion had no ready answer.

A Humanistic World

Two books appearing in 1929 had much to say about where American beliefs had been and where they might be heading: Walter Lippmann's *Preface to Morals* and Joseph Wood Krutch's *Modern Temper*. Both explained how loyalty to the traditional religions had snapped, how assurance regarding the values that they once imparted had gone. The "acids of modernity" had eaten away the purposiveness and the stabilizing certitudes, leaving in their stead an emptiness, a rootlessness, a demoralizing dismay. When the old gods fail, where does one turn? Should one seek escape through romantic or mystical flights? Should one join the sybarites of the 1920s in an anxiety-drowning chase after pleasure? Trust science for salvation? Curse God and die? Or, become a humanist?

Men who have "lost their belief in a heavenly king," wrote Lippmann, must now "find some other ground for their moral choices than the revelation of his will." Good and evil must find their authentication within human experience, not outside of it, and certainly not in the threats or seductions of hell and heaven. Virtue can never be imposed. If men do henceforth pursue virtue more than they do vice, this will only be because by personal choice and desire they prefer to do so. Such a happy choice will be made not by those seeking to do the will of God, but by those dedicated to the good of man. "When men can no longer be theists, they must, if they are civilized, become humanists." Humanism, then, can offer the direction and the drive that orthodoxy no longer provides. This "civilized" way can supply an ethic not alone for the individual; it can show all humanity the path toward happiness and well-being.

Over a long and remarkably productive career as journalist and philosopher, Walter Lippmann (b. 1889) labored to give Americans a new faith by which to live. Impatient with the thoughtless hedonism of the 1920s, convinced that old orthodoxies were gone forever, and profoundly concerned lest values worth preserving also disappear forever, Lippmann argued that modern man could not afford to become soft, self-indulgent, irrational, and immoral. Anything worthwhile in life or in civilization still required discipline and hard work. We like to think, Lippmann observed, that if all restraints on human passions were only removed, then joy and abundant living will be ours. Nonsense. One lesson the past drives home: wherever men have thought seriously about the attainment of the good, they have seen the need for sacrifice and renunciation. Asceticism of course can be irrational or passingly quaint, but "civilized asceticism" places intelligence above instinct and public weal above private pleasure.

Lippmann's respect for the past, for the wisdom of the ancients, led him to see rectitude and virtue as somehow built into the very structure of the universe. Man pursues the Good, he does not create it. Human discontent and restlessness suggest that there are standards and norms beyond the little private dramas in which each of us participates. "What is there in the back of our heads which keeps telling us that life as we find it is not what it ought to be?" Lippmann's clearest answer to that question came not in his *Preface to Morals* but a generation later in another book, *The Public Philosophy*. Here he hoped to give new vibrancy to an ancient idea: natural law. In a society that sees all truth as self-regarding and self-centered, that accepts routinely the notions that "all principles are the rationalizations of some special interest," the existence of natural law is neither readily perceived nor widely conceded. Yet a free and reasonable society cannot possibly survive unless men can see "that there are certain principles which, when they have been demonstrated, only the willfully irrational can deny; that there are certain obligations binding on all men committed to a free society, and that only the willfully subversive can reject them." Humanism, therefore, not only gives purpose and drive: it sets the limits on dissent, the borderline between sedition and radical reform being determined by the acceptance or the rejection of the idea "that we live in a rational order in which by sincere inquiry and rational debate we can distinguish the true and the false, the right and the wrong."

Drama critic, essayist, conservationist, and naturalist, Joseph Wood Krutch (1893–1970) acclaimed the possibilities of "Humanism" at the same time that he warned against all "words which are spelled with a capital letter." Krutch's own analysis of "the paradox" of humanism reveals that he takes the warning seriously. In using the term "humanism," he refers to that which sets man apart from or even above the rest of nature; at the same time, he rejects the supernatural, arguing that all satisfaction and stimulation must be found in nature itself. Moreover, when man reaches for higher virtues and a nobler toleration, he endangers a civilization that has built itself up through ruder virtues and animal passions. "Civilizations die from philosophical calm, irony and the sense of fair play quite as surely as they die of debauchery." Yet, nature's perfect societies — the ant's, for example — are made perfect by the very absence of what man thinks of as the highest humanistic values. The ant colony "owes its stability and its efficient harmony to the absence of any tendency on the part of individuals either to question the value of existence or to demand anything for themselves." It appears that social values flourish where human tendencies and concerns are in check, that humanistic values thrive only where animalistic impulses remain strong. In history, "societies are most admirable just before they collapse." It is a paradox, this humanism.

Nevertheless, it is not easy to identify more attractive alternatives. Traditional religion for Krutch as for Lippmann is finished, washed up. So faith surrenders to philosophy, and what do philosophers do? They begin "to babble of 'beneficent fictions' instead of talking about Truth," with the predictable result that men and women looking for purpose and meaning in their lives quickly lose interest. Where does hope lie? Krutch too answers that question more explicitly a generation after his *Modern Temper* appeared. In *Human Nature and the Human Condition* he observes that a world that pays more attention to the nature of the atom than it does to the nature of man is a world in need of help. When we do talk of man, Krutch wrote, it is only in terms of "norms" rather than ideals, only in terms of a standard of living and not of a "good life," only in terms of statistical averages rather than of heroic potentials. Once men believed "they were the sons of God endowed with immortal souls"; now they accept the lowest estimate of themselves — accidents of chemistry or biology, automatons of the social order. They regard

the human *condition* as the essence of human *nature*. Krutch is
unwilling to settle for so little. A "norm" must be something
more than a statistical average, something more than a synonym
for mediocrity. And that something more must find its source
and sanction in either a law of God or a law of nature. Krutch
opts for the latter. Man is, by nature, a judge and a hunter
of value; he is, by nature, discontented with mere materialism
and mere utilitarianism. Quoting Samuel Johnson, Krutch avers
that man is more than the sum of his appetites: "Prudence
and Justice are virtues and excellences of all times and of all
places; we are perpetually moralists, but we are geometricians
only by chance."

Neither Krutch nor Lippmann was willing to agree that if
God is dead, then whirl is king; they likewise rejected the bitter
consequence that if God is dead, then everything is permitted.
God is dead, but society can stand; it can even go forward to
greater goodness and glory. If the old foundation is rotted away,
new and sturdier foundations must be laid. John Dewey
(1859–1952) was humanism's chief architect for those new
foundations, for a rebuilding of the social order. Dewey, whose
humanistic bent drew more from his religious heritage and his
classical education than it did from his formal philosophy, argued
that it was high time in the 1920s and 1930s for men of good
will and good minds to address themselves to the real problems
of society. "Philosophy recovers itself when it ceases to be a
device for dealing with the problems of philosophers and becomes
a method, cultivated by philosophers, for dealing with the problems of men." Too long have "burly sinners run the world";
the time had come for the saints to get into the act. Let us
not even concern ourselves with the terms around which we
rally. Is it humanism, or naturalism, or naturalistic humanism?
No matter; "the vexatious and wasteful conflict between naturalism and humanism is terminated," along with many other pointless dualisms that have divided and distracted us. Men can make
discoveries in morals as they do in science; they can avoid dog-

matic formalism, destroy the roots of Phariseeism, and join in the
process of social growth — the only significant moral activity.
In doing all this, they need appeal neither to the laws of God nor
to the laws of nature.

God, if one insists upon restricting that word to "a particular
Being," has of course passed from the scene, Dewey grants.
However, we need to find other uses for so familiar a word.
Let us understand by the word "God" those "ideal ends that
at a given time and place one acknowledges as having authority
over his volition and emotion." With that agreement made,
we can continue to speak of God, and religion will survive as
a faith in the power of the ideal. While the historic religions
may fade away, mankind can still pursue religious ideals now
stripped of their "illusion and fancy." Similarly, with respect
to nature, one need not think in terms of eternal and absolute
"built-in" values to which men must conform. The universe
is open-ended, not closed; value systems are only plans of action,
proposed solutions to society's problems, instruments for getting
us from today's actual to tomorrow's potential. That which fosters
progress and growth, which opens up new possibilities, is ipso
facto good. All that tends to foreclose the future is, by virtue
of that fact alone, evil. The reconstruction of philosophy becomes
the reconstruction of society and the redirection of men's atten-
tions and energies from a world beyond the stars, a world we
will never know, to a world we live in and have direct responsibility for.

The humanistic sinners against faith found the pieties and
platitudes of prevailing orthodoxies obsolete. Traditional religions had lost their bite, and modern man if he was to be something more than a simpleton or a sloth had to have some other
faith by which to live. But was it enough to have a faith only
in himself, in his own capacities and powers? Bertrand Russell,
no champion of orthodoxy or tradition, thought not. Dewey
in placing both truth and value wholly in the hands of mortal
men ran some frightening risks. Dewey's challenge, said Lord

Russell, is not so much to orthodoxy as it is to the universe itself; it is a kind of a cosmic impiety, a fateful step "towards a certain kind of madness."

A Skeptical World

Even in our relaxed and latitudinarian days when religious orthodoxy no longer stabs or burns, one still harbors some trepidation in bandying about the "heretic" label. One wonders if the very last spark from all the *autos-da-fé* has really gone out, if all the dripping swords have finally been sheathed. It is with some relief, then, that we at last come to persons who revel in the accolade of heresy. Should orthodoxy be too complaisant to hurl the charge, they reach out and clutch it to their bosoms.

H. L. Mencken (1880–1956) is foremost among those dearest enemies of twentieth-century orthodoxies. As a career news-paperman, a scholarly philologist, a superb essayist, and an unrelenting iconoclast, Mencken was either the darling of Baltimore or its black beast. He permitted few pomposities cherished by his fellow citizens — the species *boobus Americanus* — to go unpunctured, few pretensions to escape unscathed. In religion, nothing was sacred. With learning and zest and with language as his agile, obedient jester, Mencken probed, jabbed, feinted, and struck home. Christianity was his favorite target and fundamentalism his special delight. Yet, as he would have quickly acknowledged, all religion was a nightmare and theology a disease. His *Treatise on the Gods*, first published in 1930, revised and increased in horsepower in 1945, served as the principal engine of his wrath.

Religion, like agriculture, is an invention of man. No justification exists, therefore, for decorating it with a lot of "metaphysical flummery" or for burdening it with elaborate explanations of its divine origin and sanction. Christianity, more irrational than most religions, appears particularly prone to take refuge in supernaturalism and absurd claims of divine revelation. If we take time to look at the holy scriptures, Mencken noted, we discover that they are a strange mishmash. The Bible is "at once a book of laws, a collection of chronicles and genealogies, and a series of prophetic tracts, hymn books, erotic rhapsodies, and primitive novels." The so-called Books of Moses reek "with irreconcilable contradictions and patent imbecilities," and New Testament writings are no better.

> The simple fact is that the New Testament, as we know it, is a hel-
> ter-skelter accumulation of more or less discordant documents, some
> of them probably of respectable origin but others palpably apocryphal,
> and that most of them, the good along with the bad, show unmistak-
> able signs of having been tampered with.

The best that one can say of the Bible as a whole is that it has a few fragments of nice Hebrew poetry in it. This is the foundation upon which the prevailing religion of the Western world is built.

If the foundation is weak, what of the structure erected upon it? In a sweep of Christian history that is breathtaking in its swiftness and its certitude, the Baltimore sage finds no improvement upon a sorry start. The early church fathers are amusing where they are not dangerous, all of them believing in "visions, prophecies, signs and portents . . . in angels, demons, dragons and leviathans." Most of them display "a great contempt for ordinary veracity." In the Middle Ages, one finds merely a more "complicated dogmatic structure, bristling with metaphysical refinements and logical impossibilities." But fortunately one need not go into the history of medieval Christianity in great detail, Mencken observes, because it has so little to do with religion.

We come quickly, then, to the Reformation, which showed some courage but not much intelligence. While the popes "roared maledictions in all directions," the Reformers kept busy fighting among themselves, producing thereby a swarm of sects and a library of theologies "quite as preposterous as that of the church of Rome." Luther was the perfect model of a theologian:

"cocksure, dictatorial, grasping, self-indulgent, vulgar and ignorant." Of Calvin one need only observe that he was the true father of Puritanism, "the worst obscenity of Western civilization." Luckily, at the same time that the Reformation was spending its furies, a movement we know as the Renaissance was ushering in the modern world. By means of growing allegiance to the Renaissance spirit, the seventeenth century managed to get rid of many "pious phantasms" while in the eighteenth century "Christian theology finally disappeared from the intellectual baggage of all really civilized men."

And that brings us to the American scene. There a growing scientific understanding of the natural world coupled with a growing skepticism regarding the supernatural world have divorced intellect from religion. ". . . if a current president of Harvard were to preach the theology of Increase Mather he would be locked up as a lunatic." Only politicians, in order to get elected, are required to repeat the discredited shibboleths. Civilized man has become his own god and Christianity in America survives, if at all, as a pale, ghostly sort of humanism. Of course, Christian theologians have not given up: they continue to break down "all the natural barriers between fact and fiction, sense and nonsense, and [convert] logic into a weapon that mauls the truth far more often than it defends it." Enlightened Americans, however, can only be skeptics; there is no other choice. As for the mob, it will continue "to live absurdly . . . and to die insanely, grasping for hands that are not there." If scarlet letters were awarded for heresy, Mencken would wear his "H" with pride.

A generation after H. L. Mencken, a Princeton philosopher, Walter Kaufmann (b. 1921), also counted himself firmly among the heretics. Skeptics found in his busy pen and his itinerant lecturing a comforting blend of brilliant documentation and steady stimulation. A native of Germany (Freiburg), Kaufmann came to the United States when seventeen years of age. Brought up a Lutheran but early turning in disbelief from that tradition

to Judaism, Kaufmann began a kind of religious quest. In his
undergraduate career (at Williams College) he considered concentrating in religion but no major was available. Since that area
of study was closed to him, he chose philosophy as his academic
major and as his career. In making that choice, however,
philosophy was seen not as a quiet, scholarly retreat from the
world. Rather, it represented a persisting life quest, a dogged
determination to be honest, a defiant resolve to resist all "enemies
of critical reason."

Among those enemies religion was to be found. In 1961 Kaufmann published *The Faith of a Heretic* revealing the scope and
nature of his quest as well as the scope and nature of his sin
against faith. To reject the traditional orthodoxies, he argued,
is not to fall into the hands of communism or of corruption
or even of indifference. The heretic can be a profoundly committed person. And because he is so thoroughly honest, his commitment may even exceed that of the orthodox. Those "who spurn
the Pablum of the pulpits" are not necessarily a lazy, contented
lot. Nor does the choice of reason as one's guide for life result
in a cool detachment and an academic aloofness. Reason is not
the enemy of commitment and academia is not a refuge from
life. Kaufmann contends, therefore, that his duties as a professor
of philosophy are consistent with his religious quest and that
his criticism of traditional religion is not mere negation or empty
iconoclasm. In order to build up, however, one must first tear
down.

For Kaufmann as for Mencken, theology in the sense of a
"science of God" simply does not exist. Instead, one has apology,
ambiguity, vested interest, and suffocating parochialism. Protestant theologians (for example, Rudolf Bultmann, Paul Tillich,
Reinhold Niebuhr) have a remarkable talent for saying "No"
in ways that sound like "Yes." At first glance Catholic
theologians appear to be more straightforward, less equivocal.
This, however, is a "first glance" only. Closer inspection reveals
that their phrases are so variously interpreted, their dogmas (for

example, papal infallibility) so ingeniously explained away, that these theologians are no more to be trusted than the Protestant variety. In truth, theology seems to be in the business of building complicated systems and convoluted exegeses that preclude a simple, clear, direct use of language. Those imposing systems, moreover, are usually constructed not for the defense of some noble truth but for the protection of some timorous sect. Theology, it must be said, "is a comprehensive, vigorous, and systematic attempt to conceal the beam in the scriptures and traditions of one's own denomination while minutely measuring the mote in the heritage of one's brothers." It is not surprising, therefore, that theology moves no mountains; in fact, "it rarely moves people."

When one uses a term like "God," all of theology's difficulties spring into view. Try to define that word and either it ascends into ethereal opacity or it descends into an intolerable crudity. Refuse to define it, and one appears to have surrendered at once to the enemy. In "A Dialogue between Satan and a Christian," Kaufmann presents the hapless believer trying to fend off the sharp, heretical queries of that fallen angel. Perhaps, says Satan, God is "not a person but a panacea, like love." As panacea he supplies so many needs: self-respect, comfort, hope, counseling center, information bureau, and final auditor and balancer of all accounts. Like love, he is everywhere. The "Christian," not wholly satisfied with the analogy, wishes to make clear that God really exists. Where, asks Satan, in space? No, the believer responds. Well, then, Satan counters, perhaps we do not really understand what is meant by "existence." Is the "existence" of God something like the "existence" of a dream, or of a concept, or of a pattern of human feelings? Or is it that you, Christian, have no more idea of what you mean by the verb "exist" than you do by the noun "God"? After much discussion, characterized by many digressions and deliberate misunderstandings, the Christian weakly concludes that he will continue to believe just what he has always believed. But, he asks distractedly, "what exactly do I believe?"

Satan is not about to answer that question, and Kaufmann is not either. In accordance with good Socratic method, the Princeton philosopher is more interested in showing the believer what he does not know, thereby provoking him to an independent and rigorous pursuit of truth. "To communicate to others some feeling for man's religious quest, to arouse an aspiration in them which nothing but death can quell, and to develop their critical powers"— this is Kaufmann's vocation. First, the idols must fall. Then let each person who will rebuild his own temple, brick by heavy brick.

In the train of Mencken and Kaufmann, not to mention their European counterparts, many Americans followed, often at some distance philologically and philosophically. Mencken's mob is not made up wholly of believers; the masses are also represented by truth-seekers, free-thinkers, evangelists for skepticism, organizers for atheism. In 1925 an American Association for the Advancement of Atheism (AAAA) received its charter from the state of New York, having been denied such on two previous occasions. Declaring itself the "Militant Foe of the Church and Clergy," AAAA set out in proper evangelical fashion to win converts by propagating its doctrines of materialism, evolution, and hedonism. The *Truth Seeker*, "oldest freethought paper in the world — founded 1873," to quote from its masthead, bound the non-believing believers together in a universal church of skepticism. Tracts, pamphlets, inexpensive handouts, and costly newspaper advertisements wooed the orthodox from their illusions with such eye-catching titles as these: "There Is No Hell," "Can We Believe in the Bible?", "No Soul! No Future Life!", "Christianity's Bloody Record," "Ditching the Deity," and in parody of scripture, "The Coward Hath Said in His Liver: There is a God." Not content with persuading its adherents to ditch the deity, organized atheism also protested presidential proclamations relating to religion, congressional legislation relating to the churches' tax exemptions, and judicial decisions demonstrating too much benevolence toward religion. The battle could be waged with confidence, however, because atheism is irresistible and the existence of God can never be proved. History, moreover, demonstrates to anyone who will examine it candidly that the belief in God, or "Godism," has at all times been accompanied "by ignorance and superstition." Whenever freedom or reform or scientific investigation move forward, it is only as Godism is forced into a shame-faced retreat. "Godism is consistent with crime, cruelty, envy, hatred, malice and uncharitableness," while atheism is identified with the opposing tendencies in the affairs of men.

Following the paths cleared by Charles Smith, Woolsey Teller, Joseph Lewis, and others, Madalyn Murray O'Hair led atheism's vigorous campaign in contemporary America. Inveighing against Bible reading and prayers in the public schools, a battle that she won, Mrs. O'Hair went on to call for an end to all tax exemptions for church property, a battle that she lost. Astronauts in outer space reading from Genesis also seemed an inappropriate activity for federal financing. In addition to extensive legal involvement, Mrs. O'Hair in 1968 began a weekly series of broadcasts from station KTBC in Austin, Texas, on the "Atheist Point of View." Heading the Society of Separationists (formed in 1966) and launching the American Atheist Press, she also edited the principal journal expounding atheist views today, *The American Atheist.* In 1969, she published a collection of her radio talks, *What on Earth is An Atheist?*, and in 1971 she supervised the reprinting of twenty-five volumes on atheism — all this as part of her bustling effort to heal America, this religion-infested land.

Dissent is always misunderstood and misrepresented, atheism especially so. Few appreciate the commendable role of freethought in America, Mrs. O'Hair writes, preferring to see all atheists as intellectual outcasts, "peculiar individuals, village idiots,

hunchbacks mad at god for having deformed them," or, in the
words of one of the Texas orthodox, even as "sneaky snarling
dogs." But atheists deserve a better press. For, if one wishes
to know the truth, they have stood for freedom and for intellectual honesty, for "fearless adherence to logic," and for practical
plans to improve the lot of society. The atheist's credo is not
altogether negative, though it does have to empty out a lot
of the trash with which so many fill their minds. That there
be no misunderstanding, Mrs. O'Hair is prepared to say just
what she does or does not believe:

> I do not believe there is a god, or any gods, personal or in nature,
> or manifesting himself, herself, or itself in any way. I do not believe
> there is such a thing as heaven, or hell, or perdition, or purgatory, or
> any other stages in between. I do not believe there is any life after
> death. I do not believe in miracles.
>   I do not believe in angels. I do not believe in prophets and I do
> not accept any holy book of any kind, be it the Bible, the Koran, the
> Torah, the Veda, the Upanishads, or anything else in any age in the
> history of man.
>   I do not believe in saviors and this includes any so-called saviors
> from Moses to Jesus Christ, or Mohammed, or his daughter Fatima, or
> Buddha, or the popes or any oracles, self-appointed or appointed by
> other persons.

All of these notions, she concludes, are silly, an insult to our
intelligence and to our common sense. And it probably would
not even be worth going into were it not for the fact that
"Religion has caused more misery to all men in every single
stage of history than any other single idea." If one counters
by saying that at least religion brings happiness to many people,
Mrs. O'Hair responds by saying that Santa Claus has done better.
   Though standing apart from the religious leaders of America,
Mrs. O'Hair in one respect stands right with them: her organization needs money. The Society of Separationists and its twenty-
eight thousand "associates" cannot alone nullify all the disastrous
effects of organized religion in America. Repeatedly the radio
talks expose how much money the churches and synagogues

receive, how much property they own, how much government favor they receive. Atheism, in contrast, needs your dollar now, P.O. Box 2117, Austin, Texas. For the hunted as for the hunter, heresy is a costly affair.

For two hundred years and more, the theme of a "Christian America" has rung from the steeples and echoed across the plains. Through all that time and across all that space, however, the theme has not gone unchallenged. The dissonances and the shrill voices are many. Speaking for the Supreme Court in 1952, Justice William O. Douglas observed that "We are a religious people whose institutions presuppose a Supreme Being." Well, perhaps. But many sinners against faith would welcome the opportunity to debate that proposition or at least to define the terms. Others would prefer simply to junk the whole dreamy idea of America as God's "new Israel," allowing Reason or Romanticism, Science or Self, Humanism, or Skepticism to have its turn in calling the tune to which society might march. Or must a society have a single tune? How many different drummers can a people hear and still walk or work together?

4

The Misfits: Sinners Against Society

Churchmen fear the schismatic and theologians abhor the heretic, but the misfit is repugnant to all. The misfit permits no vote ever to be unanimous, no assent ever to be complete. The misfit prevents those easy generalizations that society wishes to make about itself, those comfortable illusions about "the American character," "the American purpose," "the American dream." Everyone else is prepared to act, is impatient to go, but the misfit is not ready or is going the wrong way. The misfit's non-conformity appears not so much heroic as it does petty, peevish, inconvenient, and awkward.

Awkward on both sides, to be sure. The misfit himself would find life much smoother if the melting pot really did homogenize all. Yet, to allow oneself to slide gently into that absorptive mass may be to forsake all sense of identity and integrity. Accommodation to the surrounding smothering culture may mean death, at least as far as any corporate continuity is concerned. A treasured heritage, a religious thrust, a way of life — these may all be lost. A genuine counter-culture seeks not the preservation of individual eccentricity but the survival and renewal of a common life. Assimilation could make life simpler; it could also make life pointless.

In societies both closed and open, the pressures for conformity in religion are considerable. Historically, they have often been ferocious. Even in a land of religious liberty, amiable toleration, and church-state separation, the sinner against society finds his way filled with obstructions. For society has remarkable resources to draw upon in correcting its own irregularities, nullifying its contradictions, and pasting over its inconsistencies. The misfit must be alert not only for the steely sword but for the velvet glove as well. He may be exposed as an enemy or beguiled as a friend. He may be eyed with suspicion or winked at in amusement. He may be rejected from the body politic as so much foreign matter or he may be digested in the politest way. In every case the aim of the established culture is also that of the counter-culture: to preserve its identity, to insure its survival. This aim it would accomplish with as little fuss and bother as possible. If only everybody would please behave, honoring the will of the majority not only in politics but in ethics and in religion.

The Destroyed

Sometimes, the velvet glove is not enough. For the sake of the larger whole, society must deal harshly with its dissenting minorities. America's earliest misfits are still at it. In the twentieth century, as in the seventeenth, the native Indian fails to behave, at least fails to behave in a way that a culture he never knew keeps urging upon him. While Michael Wigglesworth's "hellish fiends and brutish men" are now generally spoken of in gentler terms, they are not necessarily addressed in terms of much greater understanding. In the case of the native American, dissent appeared in its most violent form, the repression of that dissent in its harshest fashion. When dealing with the conquest and decimation of the Indian, one takes refuge in the "necessities of history" and the "spirit of the people," but it is a refuge, not an explanation, far less a justification.

Early missionaries to the Indians searched eagerly for possible bridges between Indian and European cultures: theological ones (the Great Spirit), ethical ones (the Indian's restraint and discipline), even historical ones (the ten lost tribes of Israel). The frail bridges could not hold; a superior civilization saw before it a poor, benighted, pagan people. Evangelism, while destructive of Indian culture, sought to save the Indian himself from a destruction that was as sure in this world as in the next. Had assimilation been allowed, either through intermarriage or full citizenship, the process of Christianizing the native would have contributed to a peaceful accommodation and probably prevented the "ultimate" solution. Since that path was not taken, mission activity is generally seen in the dimmest light as an obtrusive, destructive invasion of the Indian's way of life. Many still fail to recognize that the alternative to civilizing and evangelizing the Indian was not anthropological purity but deception, deprivation, rejection, and extermination.

In the nineteenth century, when those alternatives became somewhat clearer, a number of civilized Americans did not hesitate to recommend the bloodier way. When the white man's push westward was met by the red man's stiffened resistance, when land lusts soared and Indian resentment rose, border battlefields were soaked with blood. In 1869 a Kansas newspaper exclaimed: "Many plans have been tried to produce peace on the border, but one alternative remains — EXTERMINATION." Restlessness, suspicion, hostility mounted as each new atrocity was reported, as each act of plunder or personal injury was noted. With unrestrained bitterness on both sides, numbers made the difference. Beginning around 1870, John Collier notes, "a leading aim of the United States was to destroy the Plains Indians societies through destroying their religions; and it may be that the world has never witnessed a religious persecution so implacable and so variously implemented." The Kansas newspaper was not a voice crying in the wilderness but an echo of national policy for dealing with dissent.

In the slaughter at Wounded Knee in South Dakota, 29 December 1890, United States soldiers killed far more Sioux women and children than they did Sioux warriors. The total

Indian losses outnumbered those of the federal military by ten to one. A different kind of numbering places the struggle of competing cultures in perspective. From 1800 to 1900, the population of the United States increased from five million to seventy-five million; in that same time period, a population of five hundred thousand Indians was reduced by half. Dissent was being destroyed.

After defeat and demoralization had come to the tribes one by one, a religious movement in the 1870s attempted to offer a straw of hope. The Ghost Dance was an effort to preserve a culture that had been trampled and to present a religious vision that deviated sharply from the Manifest Destiny of the Indian's conquerors. The Ghost Dance religion addressed itself to Indians, not to members of disparate tribes, but to a whole culture despised and rejected, to an entire people now in eclipse, a people for whom the darkness of the moment was not an eternal night. The white man's military power and his superiority of numbers is but a temporary phenomenon. The day will soon come when the mountain shall be brought low and the valley lifted up. Indians will be rejuvenated, reunited, infused with dignity and strength, as a New Age of peace, plenty, good health, and abounding joy comes to the real people. That grand reunion will include not only the Indian population now alive, but the dead will return from their spirit world (hence, the name of the dance) so that all the faithful can rejoice. An unbelieving and faithless enemy will be undone; he will be no more.

In anticipation of that good and great day — first set for the Spring of 1891 — the Indians joined in the Ghost Dance. From tribe to tribe they danced, varying the ceremony as well as the interpretation in some details, but dancing, singing, praying, and purifying in anticipation of the swift coming of that better day. Hope revived and courage returned as the dance spread from Paiute to Shoshoni to Cheyenne, Arapaho, and Sioux; believers among the Caddo, Wichita, Pawnee, and Oto also sang of a day when war would be no more.

But war remained — along with disease, starvation, expulsion, and trails of tears and death. The strong culture grew stronger, as America's oldest counter-culture grew weaker. When the Messiah did not appear, when Indian hopes were met with massacres instead of a millennium, the Ghost Dance inevitably declined. Like other men in other ages, the Indians now took another tack. If the Antichrist could not be overthrown, perhaps he could be endured. What cannot be conquered physically must be overcome spiritually. The human spirit is not made for defeat. The peyote cult became the path to spiritual victory or, if not quite victory, at least non-defeat.

Like the Ghost Dance, the peyote cult sought solidarity among all the Indians, but the unity aimed for this time was more ecclesiastical than political. If a political counter-culture could not bring in the New Age, perhaps an ecclesiastical counter-culture could. Though it was established before the Ghost Dance reached the height of its popularity, the peyote cult did not spread rapidly until that bright messianic promise began to fade. Then from the Southwest, from the Comanche and the Kiowa, the ritual use of peyote moved west and north to Arizona, Wyoming, Nebraska, Iowa, the Dakotas and even into Canada. First-century Christians who despaired of ever ridding themselves of the Roman Empire offered the council of patient suffering and steadfast faith. Nineteenth-century cultists, adopting and adapting many Christian elements, similarly turned from political aspiration to private renewal. Within the small circles of faith the sick were healed, the ignorant informed, the weak made strong, and the hopeless enabled to face the coming day. The peyote button itself (from a small, hairy, spineless cactus) granted aid and comfort against enemies without and within. In carefully prescribed ritual form, it established communion with God and with one's own fellows. It inspired belief, inculcated a pattern of behavior, and maintained a sense of community; in short, the peyote cult became a church.

On 10 October 1918, the state of Oklahoma granted to the

Native American Church its first charter. Despite opposition at the state level, uneasiness at the federal level, and uneven resistance at several ecclesiastical levels, by 1925 this new church had won a charter in six other states and by 1960 in a total of twelve. All dissent, of course, arouses resistance by the mere fact of its difference, its peculiarity, its offending nonconformity. The Ghost Dance had the added liability of representing in the minds of some a military threat to the United States of America. The peyote cult had in the minds of more the added liability of peyote itself, of *Lophophora williamsii Lemaire*. Peyote, the American public was told, was a most dangerous drug; used in moderation, it was responsible for sexual excesses and debaucheries, when used in excess it brought death. Confused for a time with mescal, peyote was also charged with being a strong intoxicant, and everyone knew what that did to the Indian. Ethnologists defending the Indian's use of the drug pointed out that, used in moderation, peyote was neither an intoxicant nor an aphrodisiac and in fact appeared to be a deterrent to alcoholic indulgence. Used to excess, peyote could well be harmful, but the same could be said of common table salt or coffee or ordinary tobacco. In conditions controlled by the group, peyote was not addictive, was not harmful. Perhaps, the defenders added, it should be compared with another item used by the Indians to the South, quinine; there, too, both ecclesiastical and political authorities tried to stamp out its use until the white man discovered that it was good for him as well.

The extensive debate over the use of peyote, a debate carried on mainly among the whites, was occasionally augmented by the direct testimony of the Indians. Native Americans pointed out the purely religious uses of peyote and noted the high moral standards maintained by its users. Those who went seeking great orgies among the peyote-users returned disappointed. Moreover, the peyote cult, unlike the Ghost Dance, was an effort at accommodation to the dominant culture. The Native Church in Nebraska, for example, indicated that spirit in its politic explanation of peyote's religious role:

We believe in the sacrament and the sacramental bread and wine, but in so much as the use of the same is forbidden to Indians, we . . . have adopted the use of Peyote as bread and water as wine.

The peyote button as the body of Christ: how could a Christian culture extirpate that? The firmest protection for the peyote cult, however, lay in its claim to First Amendment rights for the free exercise of religion. The creation of the Native American Church was inspired, in part, by the hope that America would honor freedom for religion even though it had dishonored freedom of the Indian. Under the protective mantle of religion, perhaps dissent could survive; perhaps some uniquely Indian contribution to the spiritual quest, some fragment from the Indian's past, could be preserved. That confidence appeared justified as opposition to the cultic use of peyote died down in the later 1920s and as the Indian Bureau under John Collier in the 1930s became more the Indian's defender than his attacker.

In the 1960s, however, because of rising anxieties about drugs in the total youth culture of America, peyote again came under attack. Arrests were made and court challenges heard. In 1960 an Arizona state court ruled that peyote was legal for bona fide members of the Native American Church. In 1962 three Navajos were arrested in California for using peyote in a religious rite held in a desert hogan near Needles. Charged with violation of the California narcotics act, the Navajos were found guilty, the lower court seeing in the free exercise of religion clause no defense for a clearly illegal act. The California Supreme Court reversed that decision (*People* v. *Woody*, 1964), asserting that the protection of religious freedom did in this instance outweigh the state's "compelling interest." On the federal level, meanwhile, the Drug Abuse Control Act was amended to include peyote and other psychedelic (literally, "mind-expanding") drugs. First the sale and then even the possession of peyote became illegal. Despite these federal actions, judicial authorities, at least for the moment, are disposed to treat the Native American Church as a legitimate exception to the general operation of these laws. These sinners against society, these members of a church that "doesn't look like a church"— some quarter-million of them — have avoided destruction for a time. They have won the right to pursue spiritual realities in their own way among their own people in the context of their own historic traditions. They look for Truth not in a book or a creed or an external event but in the heights or depths of their own souls.

The Exiled

For so much of American history freedom has meant a freedom to move on. An empty wilderness beckoned or lured. This observation of Sidney Mead's might be augmented to include another dimension of American history: the freedom to tell the other fellow to move on. Whether violence is as American as cherry pie, exile — voluntary and otherwise — surely is. In the spaciousness of the North American continent a favorite way to solve a social problem was simply to declare it "off limits." Colonial Virginians ran off the Puritans, while New England Puritans ran off the Quakers, the Baptists, the Anglicans, and itinerant preachers of any stripe. Jews were ejected from Manhattan, Huguenots from Florida, and Roman Catholics from just about everywhere. While many American colonies were havens from a European persecution of religion, the colonies themselves withdrew or circumscribed hospitality each after its own fashion. With good reason the line, "And never darken my door again!" became a cliché of village drama in America.

Quite early in its history, Massachusetts, for example, found exile a convenient instrument. Roger Williams's stubborn dissent posed an unnerving threat to the young Bay Colony. Trying

to form a true church of Christ in the wilderness, Williams
protested a government that demanded religious conformity in
a popish manner, that compromised the independence of local
congregations, that deceived itself in its strange reluctance to
break cleanly from the Church of England, that trespassed on
land that really belonged to the Indians. Massachusetts, it
appeared, had managed to do little that was right. From that
colony's point of view, the greatest error it had committed was
to put up with Roger Williams. Not to compound that crime,
Massachusetts indicated that its hospitality was at an end. To
so rude and ungracious a guest, therefore, the Massachusetts
authorities decreed in October 1635, "that the said Mr. Williams
shall depart out of this jurisdiction." Exile was the solution:
an immediate exile to the wilderness if he kept on preaching,
a delayed exile the following spring to England if he could manage to keep quiet. Williams could not quite manage to keep
still. Consequently, in the middle of winter, Williams was
ordered out and away, beyond the borders, beyond the pale.
For fourteen weeks "sorely tossed" and "not knowing what bread
or bed did mean," Williams wandered southward, making his
way to the headwaters of Narragansett Bay. There he bought
some land from the Indians and founded the village of Providence
"in a sense of God's merciful providence to me in my distress."
The colony of Rhode Island and Providence Plantations, begun
by an exiled dissenter, became a haven for other misfits, seekers,
mystics, prophetesses, and the disaffected. Not only New England but New York as well found Rhode Island a convenient
dumping ground for guests no longer welcome, for problems
not otherwise readily solved.

    In 1654 Peter Stuyvesant, keeping an anxious eye upon the
motley immigrants coming into his New Amsterdam, was dismayed to see even Jews arriving in the small struggling colony.
To the directors of the Dutch West India Company, founders
of the settlement, Stuyvesant explained that the presence of the
Jews was "very repugnant" because of their present poverty and

their persisting reputation for "deceitful trading" and charging
high rates of interest. "For the benefit of this weak and newly
developing place and the land in general," Stuyvesant therefore
decided "to require them in a friendly way to depart." The gover-
nor added his hope that such "hateful enemies and blasphemers"
not be allowed anytime in the future to "infect and trouble"
the colony but that this exile be a permanent exclusion. In this
hope Stuyvesant was to be disappointed. The directors of the
company overruled him and New Amsterdam's earliest Jewish
arrivals were permitted to stay, forming the oldest synagogue
community in America. Other colonial synagogues arose in
Rhode Island (Newport), Pennsylvania (Philadelphia), South
Carolina (Charleston), and Georgia (Savannah).

So the Stuyvesant plan of exile did not work. Nevertheless,
for dissenters so persistent in their dissent, for misfits so unwilling to be melted, the established order found other ways to
say "never darken my door again." Prior to the Civil War the
Jewish population in America, well under one hundred thousand
persons, was if not meltable hardly yet visible. In the final decade
of that century, however, the numbers ascended swiftly to one
million, and to five times that many one-half century later. This
eastern European immigration, overwhelming the earlier entry
of Spanish, Portuguese, and German Jewry, comprised a dissenting bloc that was visible indeed. The visibility was more than
a matter of mere numbers. For the emigrants from eastern Europe
had even less interest in accommodation and assimilation than
did their German counterparts. What to do with or about such
an undigestible chunk in the social organism? At a minimum
it seemed prudent to retard or cut off the flow of foreignness
into America. Restrictive immigration laws of 1921 and the
National Origins Act in 1924 were important and effective
instruments of that purpose.

This technique, a kind of exile-before-the-fact, did not solve
the problem of those already arrived, and a western wilderness
had moved too far away to be immediately available. These dis-

senters resisted conversion as well as assimilation; they were too
numerous to ignore and too entrenched to be moved. They were,
clearly, a threat. In his *Dearborn Independent*, Henry Ford probed
for an alternative method of dealing with America's Jews. From
1920 to 1927 he indicted them all as participants in world-wide
conspiracies. Giving both credence and prestige to the nation's
first feverish swell of anti-Semitism, Ford even provided the
general public with its first taste of the *Protocols of the Learned
Elders of Zion*. And he helped Michigan become receptive to
other demagoguery: for example, Gerald L. K. Smith who left
his Louisiana base in 1935 to carry on in the North his ugly
crusade.

The *Protocols*, purportedly a Jewish blueprint for taking over
the world, was actually a clever fabrication of the Russian pro-
Czarist secret police. The document revealed how through
revolution, social disorder, and financial control a Jewish world
dictatorship would come into being. Since the Jews received
here full credit for the Bolshevik revolution of 1918, American
readers of the *Dearborn Independent* found their fear of communism
blending with their anxiety over a growing Jewish minority.
Protocol 1 declared that despotism must be encouraged since
"only force conquers in political affairs" and since the savage
mob is but a collection of "alcoholized animals." Communism
is inevitable because we Jews "shall create . . . a universal
economic crisis" in which the people will take to the streets
destroying and looting the property of those "they have envied
from their cradles. . . ." The religion of the Gentiles, furthermore, must be destroyed, their faith in God undermined. In
its place will stand a dedication to industry, trade, "arithmetical
calculations and material needs." By lies, cruelty, re-education
and above all power, the descendants of King David will rise
once more to rule the whole earth. However extreme a document,
the *Protocols* was not too wild to be believed in the midst of
Red scares and un-Christian dissent.

If the Jew cannot be cast out, perhaps he can be made an

outcast. The pariah can remain in our midst, but only at arm's length. In the late 1930s, again in Michigan, the publications and radio broadcasts of Father Charles E. Coughlin sought to maintain or extend that social distance. In his weekly newspaper, *Social Justice*, Coughlin began the republication of the *Protocols* in July 1938, avowing that he was not so much interested in their authenticity as "in their factuality." In November of that year, he started using the radio in his anti-Semitic campaign to awaken and alert an American public "mesmerized by British gold and Jewish propaganda." By means of his "Christian Front" organization and his considerable eloquence, this Roman Catholic embarrassment parroted much of Hitler's propaganda against the Jew. Like a Protestant embarrassment, Gerald B. Winrod, organizer of the "Defenders of the Christian Faith," Father Coughlin saw the war against communism as a religious crusade. And he saw communism, along with other ills of the modern world, as a Jewish responsibility. *Social Justice* reached about a million readers at the height of its popularity, while the radio broadcasts from Coughlin's Royal Oak parish reached countless more. America's entry into World War II had been engineered by the Jews, Coughlin pointed out, as Franklin D. Roosevelt fell captive to his Jewish advisers. We are plunged "into a seething cauldron of bloody war for the protection of 600,000 racialists or religionists as you care to call them . : ."; such a war is not worth fighting. By the time this war engulfed America, Coughlin had reached the peak of his influence. The limits of ecclesiastical forebearance having also been reached (Pius XII, unlike Pius XI, "was no friend of mine"), he was silenced in 1942, and anti-Semitism had to search for other champions at home.

Abroad, no search was necessary. Hitler's calculated genocide, partially concealed during the war years themselves, was revealed in its awesome horror in the stench of Dachau, Auschwitz, Buchenwald, and other extermination camps. Dissent there met its blackest fate. In the United States during and following

World War II, the raucous hate-mongering never wholly died
but its decibel level was lowered. Within the middle and upper-
class establishments, discrimination against the Jew became
genteel, subtle, covert. In the literature of the Gentile have-nots,
the spirit of a Coughlin or Winrod or Ford (who later recanted
his anti-Semitism) lived on. Meanwhile, the dissenting voice
of the surviving Jews in America grew stronger. In literature
and the arts, in politics and religion, Jews cried out against
the insane inhumanities of man to other men and against man's
insidious dehumanization of himself.

   In these difficult, painful years the strongest religious voice
lifted in dissent was that of Rabbi Stephen S. Wise (1874–1949).
After a period as a young minister in Portland, Oregon, Wise
in 1906 returned to New York City to lead a newly established
Free Synagogue. Thus, like Theodore Parker a century before,*
he was at liberty to follow a sensitized conscience and a full
heart wherever they might lead. Civil rights, religious rights,
the special needs of children, the reform of local government,
the Zionist cause, the Hitler menace, the bigotry of fellow
Americans — these and a host of other causes Wise gave himself
to without reservation. "For me," he said, "the supreme declaration of our Hebrew Bible was and remains: 'Justice, justice,
shalt thou pursue' whether it be easy or hard, whether it be
justice to white or black, Jew or Christian." Often joining with
"my beloved friend" John Haynes Holmes, Unitarian pastor in
New York City, Wise not only helped religious dissent to find
its voice, for half a century he encouraged a nation to find its
moral bearings. At times it appeared that it was society itself
that did not "fit"; only the dissenters knew where the center
of civilization was to be found.

   Exile to the wilderness of Rhode Island, exile to the loneliness
of the ghetto or the agonies of self-doubt, exile to a rapidly
receding West — Americans followed all three courses in
"disposing" of dissent. The third pattern was employed for the

*See above, p. 55f.

Church of Jesus Christ of Latter-Day Saints. Out of Fayette, New York, Joseph Smith moved his tiny community in 1831 to Kirtland, Ohio. Hoping for even more freedom on the still advancing frontier, Smith directed a Mormon colonizing effort in western Missouri. In the summer of 1833, however, the non-Mormons resolved to rid themselves, "peaceably if we can, forcibly if we must," of these "fanatics or knaves" who attempted to live among them. The Mormons moved in without property or substance, claiming that God had given them the land, but the non-Mormons responded that "we are not prepared to give up our pleasant places and goodly possession to them. . . ." If one needed more reason for opposition to the newcomers, Mormon theology provided it, for their doctrine, "derogatory to God and religion," was dedicated "to the utter subversion of human reason." Rumors that the Mormons pursued an inclusive racial policy further aggravated the fears of frontier Missourians. The solution: exile. From Jackson County to Clay County; from Clay, Van Buren, and Lafayette counties to Ray County, and from there to a county formed by Mormons themselves, named with faint hope, "Far West."

But these exiles were as nothing. Experience in migration was still that of the amateur. Having attempted settlements in yet other areas of Missouri, Mormons found their neighbors unrelenting; they also found the cost in suffering and in property unbearable. In 1838, therefore, the saints petitioned the legislature of Missouri for redress of their many grievances. The state, in response, called out the militia to banish all Mormons — twelve thousand or so — from their land. By the middle of 1839 the exile from Missouri was accomplished, and the following year all remnants, including those left behind in Ohio, gathered along the Mississippi in western Illinois in the newly founded town of Nauvoo. Once again, the Mormons set about creating a cohesive community and perchance a perfect society; they built a temple, organized a defensive force, and established a government. Four years later, in 1844, Joseph Smith was assassinated as the hospitality of Illinois proved even more of a foolish fancy than that of Missouri. In an effort to forestall more bloodshed, Brigham Young as Smith's successor determined that the next exile would be voluntary. In 1845 he informed the authorities of Illinois that "a general exodus in the spring" of 1846 would occur. To his fellow dissenters, he said: "The exodus of the nation of the only true Israel from these United States to a far distant region of the west, where bigotry, intolerance and insatiable oppression lose their power over them, forms a new epoch, not only in the history of the church, but of this nation." Like that other, older Israel, the Mormons found in persecution and exile the fires of purification and preservation. By the time the often-dispersed Mormons reached the Salt Lake valley in Utah Territory, the survival of an American-made dissent was insured. A desert bloomed, a State of Deseret prospered, an energetic, disciplined church did indeed enter upon a new epoch.

In one respect, however, the battle for dissent was lost. The Mormon's most notorious sin against society, polygamy, had to be abandoned. More a social sin than a federal offense, polygamy was deemed unacceptable in Western civilization generally and in American civilization specifically. As the United States Supreme Court carefully explained in 1890, polygamy "is contrary to the spirit of Christianity and of the civilization which Christianity has produced in the Western world. . . . The state has a perfect right to prohibit polygamy, and all other offenses against the enlightened sentiment of mankind. . . ." While conceding that round to the forces of consent, the Mormons in virtually every other respect found, in their final exile, the time and space and vision to win a geographically dramatic victory for dissent. This new Israel, in its theology and its social patterns, its missionary aggressiveness and its economic strength, did mark a new epoch in the history of the nation, as Brigham Young had predicted.

Eventually, Manifest Destiny ran out of space. When that happened, the methods for dealing with the sinners against society had to undergo further refinement or develop a subtler complexity.

The Feared

The sinners against society most feared are the deniers of the American dream. These dissenters speak more of national failure than of national success; they perceive in the nation more low self-gratification than high moral purpose; they turn more to despair than to hope. In their field of vision the American dream appears as a nightmare. A society suckled on that dream reacts with fear that borders on panic or hysteria, for a proud America does not treat lightly any tampering with its divine destiny. Hubris is always an unsteady state.

In *The American Idea of Mission*, Edward McNall Burns nicely summarizes the basic propositions in the American self-image. Americans have a duty "to proclaim liberty throughout the world and to all the inhabitants thereof." Second, America as a society without titles of honor or hobbling traditions must exemplify the virtues of equality among all its citizenry. Third, "America is the home of the truest and most complete democracy to be found in the world." As a nation under civilian control, moreover, this land must always be an apostle for peace and an opponent of militarism. Finally, enjoying the world's highest standard of living, America is called upon to share its blessings with all mankind. In such terms the dominant culture sees itself; this destiny of America is as glorious as it is assured. Would any dissenter, in the name of God, dare to shorten his nation's heavenly reach?

Most religiously oriented Americans have of course joined in and even promoted that confident view of the American future. God has a plan for this nation, a task for her to perform. The American way and the Christian way are not antithetical; for some they have been identical. The prophet called to transform society becomes its advocate and apologist. The vision of that

day "when the saints go marching in" gets confused with national
interests and Pentagon policies. Transcendent loyalties and political duties contest against each other briefly, until one learns
that no conflict of interest really exists. The judgments of the
churches and synagogues turn out to be endorsements, as the
culture captures all. Exceptions, however, do exist. And when
cultural criticism appears to be not simply the eccentricity of
an overheated zealot but the steady determination of a party
or a sect, then unease or fear sets in.

Black nationalism challenges the American dream. In its
religious dimension, it severs that powerful partnership between
Christian hope and national aspiration. The contemporary black
Muslim did not invent but only caps a long disturbing tradition
of black religious nationalism in America. Separate "African"
churches in the land, sustained efforts to abandon this land
because it is not and never will be "our land," and other group
endeavors made the point that America's cultural hold was really
a death grip for blacks. Black clergymen led the way in asserting
a separate hope and a separate destiny. Alexander Crummell,
for example, thought it folly for blacks to assume that because
they were American citizens they would therefore "share in the
common heritage and destiny of the nation." On the contrary,
this able Episcopal rector from Washington, D.C., noted in
1875 that blacks are a " 'peculiar people' in this land; looked
at, repulsed, kept apart, legislated for, criticized . . . at an
intolerable and insulting distance *as* a peculiar people." That
being the case, black men and women have no choice but to
organize and unite among themselves "for effective action and
for the noblest ends." Rather than try to forget that they are
colored, blacks had best remember it every minute: "what this
race needs in this country is *power* — the forces that may be
felt." To this call for separatist unity, Bishop Henry M. Turner
of the African Methodist Episcopal Church in the same decade
added his own voice, urging particularly a return to Africa.
America, he noted, promises freedom but never grants it, talks

of political rights but never permits their full exercise. It is
time to demand an indemnity for centuries of servitude and
leave this land, "for Africa is our home, and is the one place
that offers us freedom and manhood."

These nineteenth-century dissents in the name of religion
attracted little attention. In the twentieth century, however,
Black Muslims won the attention and therewith the anxiety of
that other nine-tenths of the nation's population. Rejecting
Christianity as the religion of the white man, the Nation of
Islam slowly built up its strength in the 1930s and 1940s. By
the 1950s and after, Black Muslims had become front-page copy.
The general public had opportunity to read the proclamations
of Elijah Muhammad (b. 1897), who has led the Muslims since
1933; the public, or its children, read the widely popular
Autobiography of Malcolm X, the dynamic leader (1925–1965)
who served the Muslim cause from 1952 to 1964; and that public
watched the boxer Muhammad Ali (b. 1943), who claimed
exemption from the military draft on the grounds of his status
as a Muslim clergyman, do much of his fighting against the
nation's courts. From these and other sources a contented culture
learned a different view of the world: the black man has a great
heritage and an even greater destiny. The first has been deliberately concealed and the second cruelly frustrated by the white
man, who is the very personification of evil. Black, Allah's original creation, is altogether beautiful and good; white, a weaker
hybrid of the primitive stock, is altogether vicious and inferior.
The superior mental, moral, and physical stature of the black
race has been systematically subverted by satanic Caucasians for
six thousand years and, in America, for four hundred years. In
this unnatural and vile reversal, the Christian religion has been
the eager partner and the master strategist, teaching among other
things that God desires the black man to be the white man's
slave. "The Bible," said Elijah Muhammad, "is the graveyard
of my poor people." All in all, it did not sound much like
the authorized version of the American dream.

Considering all that a white, Christian nation has done to
the black man for centuries past, what can this long-abused
man expect from such a society in the future? Nothing but more
degradation and exploitation and deception and blood. The best
course for the black, therefore, is to keep himself as untainted
and as distant as possible. The last course to follow is one of
seeking "acceptance" into white society. Segregation, not integration, is the goal. One must work not for ultimate assimilation
but for immediate identity and integrity of the black race, the
"so-called Negro." To that end, all intermarriage must cease,
all pollution of black blood must stop. Integration is merely
another white man's trick as he attempts to keep black men
from realizing that their time in history has come at last. The
separation of black from white must ultimately, of course, be
territorial. It is time for America to divide the land with her
slaves. Twenty million blacks, said Elijah Muhammad, call for
a land of their own, a distinct territory. One or two states,
perhaps four or five; Malcolm X suggested that possibly "nine
or ten states would be enough." "Why can't the black man
in America have a piece of land," Malcolm X asked, "with
technical help and money to get his own nation established?
What's so fantastic about that? We fought, died and helped
to build this country, and since we can't be citizens here, then
help us to build a nation of our own."

This "black Zionism" strikes at national unity in the most
direct manner possible. Who can think of Louisiana and Mississippi, of Alabama and Georgia, or of other states as going to
another nation? Can Manifest Destiny reverse itself? Should the
course of empire voluntarily become a dead end? In his *Message
to the Blackman in America*, Elijah Muhammad in 1965 declared
that only one solution existed to the domination of Christianity
and of its organizers, the white race. That solution, Allah has
shown, is to have some land. Nations are only recognized as
such because they occupy a specific area of the earth. The same
will be true of the Nation of Islam. Millions of blacks deserve

to be, must be, a nation; otherwise they will be exploited slaves and fawning Uncle Toms forever. "We cannot be successful in the house of our enemies; we should be in our own house." Blacks have the skills, the intelligence, and the capacity in every way to be a self-governing nation. If they do not have the vision to become such, it is only because they do not understand that Allah is on their side and will fight for them. The time came when the Hebrews had to be separated from Egypt, and woes fell upon Egypt for trying to prevent that God-appointed deliverance. America will be cursed if she tries to prevent a new nation from coming into being, a new nation under Allah with liberty and justice — finally — for all. Blacks will be cursed if they continue to believe the old lie that Christianity teaches love for all men. Only one message does Elijah Muhammad have for his people: Separate and be saved. Only one message for America: Let my people go.

In all of nature, the principle of territoriality runs deep. To strike out against the integrity of the land is to launch a frontal assault upon the sovereignty of the nation itself. And to make this battle an anti-Christian crusade is to shatter a Messianic vision as well as a political dream. All the anxieties and phobias of race, religion, and patriotism are brought to boil. "Repent," cried Malcolm X, "repent, America." Should America refuse to repent, then Allah will do to it as was done to the wicked kingdoms of old. Allah "will erase the American government and the entire race that it favors and represents from this planet. . . . [He] will then give the whole earth back to the original owners, the black man!" Americans, however, did not repent. They just grew fearful, the depth of their fear being checked by the recognition that Elijah Muhammad never really spoke for twenty million blacks, perhaps for fewer than 1 percent of that number. It was not necessary, at least not yet, to hold huge public rallies, to organize counter-crusades, to elect officials pledged to oppose the "Muslim threat," or to engage in any number of other activities called for when fear becomes hysteria.

With Marxism, the response was different. Challenges to free enterprise, property rights, and profits invariably invoked the strongest response and the most highly organized counterattacks. The challenges did not even have to be genuinely Marxist, certainly not part of a foreign communist conspiracy, to arouse the deepest antipathies. It was often enough to favor the worker over the owner, to criticize the government's alliance with business, or to suggest that capitalism was something less than Christianity in economic dress. The issue of territorial integrity was serious; the integrity of the economic system was an issue of cosmic proportion. In that sacred realm dissent trod on its most dangerous ground and religion, even Christianity, could be seen for the first time as destiny's enemy, not its ally.

What a perverse partnership "Christian Marxism" was — a linking of righteousness with iniquity, of light with darkness, of Christ with Belial. In the darkest days of America's economic depression, however, that bond was forged. When an influential Methodist leader such as Harry F. Ward embraced Marxism and denounced *Our Economic Morality* (1929), the sleeping shades of fear and mutual suspicion stirred. A socially relevant Christianity raised so many specters in the 1930s that even a generation later "social Christianity" represented to many a betrayal both of nation and of faith. Reinhold Niebuhr (1892–1971), Protestantism's most publicized spokesman for a religion applied to the problems of society, saw Marxism in the 1930s as offering useful insights into the harsh realities of modern economic life. The weaknesses, even more, the perversities of capitalism destined it not for glory but for decay and defeat. The aches and ills of the Great Depression spoke with their own eloquence of the deficiencies of western economic patterns, even as they gave credence to the validity of the Marxist critique. In 1935, Niebuhr wrote:

We believe that a capitalistic society is destroying itself and yet that it must be destroyed, lest it reduce, in the delirium of its disintegration, our whole civilization to barbarism. We believe that social

ownership of the means of production is the only basis of health and
justice for a technical age. We believe that such a society can be established only through a social struggle and that in that struggle we
ought to be on the side of the workingman. In these things we support socialism wholeheartedly.

Liberal Protestants had too long shared with most other
Americans the comfortable illusion that progress was inevitable.
Sentimentalists all, we tell men to love, to imitate Christ, and
all will be well. But Christ loved, and all was not well: he
ended up on a cross. Realism, said Niebuhr, is called for, not
naïve idealism. In a world of mammoth power structures and
heartless economic forces, a soft-headed theology simply would
not do. Niebuhr found that kind of naïveté unhelpful as he
tried to minister to a parish in Detroit, the very heart of indus-
trial America. Later, from his post at Union Theological Semi-
nary in New York City, he continued to inveigh against a
theology of consent and against an establishment America. Most
theologians and most Americans were unwilling to admit the
brutal power of self-interest, unwilling to acknowledge the vi-
ciousness inherent in capitalism, unwilling to grant the working
man his share in the system's bounty, and above all unwilling
to seek justice with a cold eye and a steady hand.

Justice must be the highest ethical aim for groups, as love
is the ethical ultimate for individuals. In *Moral Man and Immoral
Society*, published in 1932, Niebuhr called on his countrymen
to distinguish clearly "between the moral and social behavior
of individuals and of social groups — national, racial, and
economic." Relationships between groups are always political
rather than ethical, with power more than morality the determi-
nant of each group's success or failure. We employ all sorts
of reasons to defend our actions, but these may merely be dis-
guises of the egoistic impulse — an impulse of great strength
within the individual but of enormous power in the group.
Nations, for example, hold themselves together more by force
and emotion than by ethical principle or reason. Unable to

engage in any self-criticism, nations do not readily accept the
criticism of others; "nations crucify their moral rebels with their
criminals upon the same Golgotha." Committed to a placid and
undemanding moral mediocrity, nations are unable to distinguish between those whose idealism transcends that mediocrity
and those whose avarice brings them short of it. When economic
privilege and political power are allied, as in capitalism, then
national greed is at its worst and exploitation at its most vicious.
If men must have a ruling class, capitalistic or communistic,
the latter "would seem to be preferable in the long run" since
communist rulers would have no private economic interest to
set against the economic interest of the whole.

If Niebuhr was Marxist at this stage in his development, he
was nonetheless Christian. Beginning with sharp criticisms of
Christian illusions, he moved to increasingly sharp criticisms
of Marxist illusions. Marxism's vision of a classless utopia, he
came to see, was as naïve and sentimental as anything that liberal
Protestantism had ever put forward. Furthermore, Marxism's
total embrace of materialism obscures the dual nature of man,
who in fact does not live by bread alone, and rejects any transcendental dimension to the universe. The Communist vision of a
coming kingdom, totally within history and totally within man's
grasp, leads to a tyranny and a fanaticism fully as frightening
as the most extravagant schemes of religious zealots. Unrestrained
and irresponsible power is terrifying, no matter by whom wielded
or under what banner exercised. By 1940, therefore, Niebuhr
had become a perceptive critic of the Marxist world view. He
remained, however, a steady dissenter against much in American
society and in American religion. And he continued to argue
for a clear separation of the Christian hope from the American
dream. Perhaps we are a "very religious" people, but if so only
in the same sense that Paul told the Athenians that they too
were "very religious." Among both Athenians and Americans
a great deal of religious noise can be heard, a great deal of religious
bustle can be observed. Yet, we like those ancients pay homage

to all sorts of gods and scant attention to God. "Our religiosity seem to have as little to do with the Christian faith as the religiosity of the Athenians." Niebuhr's Marxist phase concluded, his phase as Christian misfit and dissenting gadfly persisted to the end of his life.

Another dissenting voice, also heard steadily from the 1930s into the 1970s, emanated from Roman Catholicism. Dorothy Day (b. 1898), like Niebuhr, was attracted to, challenged by, and then alienated from the Marxist perspective. Following her conversion to Roman Catholicism in 1927, Day saw more Marxist than Christian concern on behalf of America's working classes and her poor. Together with a French Roman Catholic layman, Peter Maurin, she founded a monthly periodical in 1933, the *Catholic Worker.* In obvious imitation of, and response to, the Communist *Daily Worker,* "Catholic Worker" seemed almost as strange a yoking together as "Christian Marxist." The strangeness was not minimized by Dorothy Day's paper making its first appearance on May Day, 1933, in New York City's Union Square. Writing long after the event, Dwight MacDonald commented: "The Marxist natives couldn't classify this political chimaera: its forequarters were anarchistic but its hinder parts were attached to the Church of Rome, whose American hierarchy then stood slightly to the right of Herbert Hoover." Without clerical leadership or hierarchical blessing, this penny-a-copy paper rapidly rose to a peak circulation of around 150,000 by the end of the 1930s.

If Marxist natives were puzzled by the anatomical peculiarities of the *Catholic Worker*, other natives were bemused by a dedication to poverty so consistent as to keep the publishing house itself perennially impoverished. No salaries were paid, no subscriptions canceled, no monies accepted for hospitality and charity extended throughout New York City. The hungry were fed and the afflicted were comforted as the Christian ethic descended from its lofty abstraction to become a simple way of life. We come to know God, Dorothy Day wrote, "in the breaking of the bread, and we know each other in the breaking of the bread, and we are not alone any more." Out of poverty came community and out of community came love: "the final word is love."

It is time, the first issue of the *Worker* declared, for a Catholic paper on behalf of the unemployed to appear. It is time for the hungry and homeless to know "that the Catholic church has a social program." It is time to reject the notion that "radical" is inevitably the ally of atheist, and time to consider the notion that "radical" and "religious" might be a fruitful conjunction. "Is it not possible to protest, to complain, to point out abuses and demand reforms without desiring the overthrow of religion?" Assuming the answer to that query to be an affirmative one and taking their texts from the promising encyclicals of Leo XIII (*Rerum novarum*, 1891) and Pius XI (*Quadragesimo anno*, 1931), Dorothy Day and her fellows challenged an American economic system so soon grown callous and cruel, challenged a Church so late in joining faith to justice.

Everything printed in that little paper, whether editorial or reportorial, was designed to keep the need for social justice before the reader: the plight of the Negro, the misery of the sweatshops, the eviction of the unemployed, the power of the Ku Klux Klan, the threats to world peace, the exploitation of sharecroppers, coal miners, textile workers, and child laborers. The most distinctive quality of this journalistic venture, however, were the Catholic Workers themselves, all deeply and personally involved in the fight for justice. They provided justice where they could and, where they could not, they did everything possible to mitigate the consequences of injustice. The Houses of Hospitality, about thirty of them in all, became an integral part, a growing and begging part, of the Catholic Worker movement. (With not a hint of apology, a 1934 *Worker* editorial, having asked for beds, books, foods, blankets, and cash, concluded: "A great many of our friends urge us to put our business on a businesslike basis. But this isn't a business, it's a movement. And we don't know anything around here about business anyway.") Catholic social action was not so much to be debated as it was to be done. Cooperatives sprang up, protest marches were led, and boycotts were called. All of this and more was done on the most direct, immediate level of individual responsibility. Christian charity was too real and too compelling to be lost in a fog of rhetoric or evaded in a shuffle of bureaucratic organization. "We just went out and *did* things. We didn't form a Committee to Promote Improved Interracial Relations. We took Negroes in our homes and lived with them."

Savonarola could call for reform as much as he wished, until some persons actually began to take him seriously. Dissent then became intolerable. The *Catholic Worker's* call for Christian charity and apostolic poverty did not frighten, but acting out that charity and voluntarily embracing that poverty could well be another matter. To that kind of persuasive personification, people might listen; they might even follow an example so clearly set. Here were unordained men and women who, without benefit of market analysis or legislative mandate or public funding or ecclesiastical direction, simply went about doing good. Thus Father Coughlin's anti-Semitism was condemned in print and counteracted in practice. Thus war was denounced in the pacifist 1930s, but with equal force it was denounced in the nonpacifist 1940s. Thus editors were hauled off to jail and Dorothy Day was hustled off to the Women's House of Detention as the tolerance for pacifism diminished. Subscriptions declined and poverty remained, but then the "business" was never expected to succeed. The movement only claimed that social justice was not a slogan but a life, and that Christian compassion could never be punched out and fed to a computer.

Neither Reinhold Niebuhr nor Dorothy Day is feared any longer: they frightened and awakened an earlier generation. Nonetheless, the tradition in which they stood, that of a socially sensitive, even radical, religious left, has lost none of its capacity to alarm. In the 1950s, at the height of the Joseph McCarthy era, dozens of clergymen were denounced as pinks, dupes, fellow

travelers, starry-eyed do-gooders, or even as agents of the enemy.
An Air Force training manual suggested that clerical ranks were
thoroughly infiltrated by subversives. After that hysteria passed,
anxieties subsiding for a time rose again in the 1960s when
priests, rabbis, ministers, and nuns protested domestic policies
that discriminated and degraded and foreign policies that
decimated and destroyed. If we leave Southeast Asia too soon,
we are told, we will lose face. Very well, responded Rabbi
Abraham Heschel, we can stay and lose our soul. In 1970 Father
Daniel Berrigan, S.J., was arrested for an alleged plot related
to his opposition to America's involvement in Vietnam. After
months of eluding the Federal Bureau of Investigation, he was
finally taken into custody on Block Island, off the coast of Rhode
Island. The anxious frown on the face of the arresting FBI agent
contrasted with the calm joy of the dissenter. A photograph
taken of that scene moved Robert McAfee Brown, a Presbyterian
clergyman and himself a persistent dissenter, to write:

> *The FBI, image all fractured,*
> *Rode out after Dan, unenraptured.*
> *They returned from the ride,*
> *A grim Fed at Dan's side*
> *And a smile on the face of the captured.*

Religious dissent could still arouse fear, and fear could still call
for force to silence dissent.

The Ridiculed

Philosophies of history are not readily refuted. Bogged down
in the stream of events, we mere mortals do not find it easy
to detect the stream's source or perceive its distant end. It is
far simpler, therefore, to praise that view of history that is agreeable to the times, and to ridicule that which is out of touch
and unfashionable. Currently, a proclamation of the world's
impending doom and catastrophic destruction is not — despite
the advent of nuclear energy — à la mode. Millennialism is out,

at least in that form that foresees the world ending with apocalyptic (and apoplectic) suddenness. Trumpets may blow, battles may rage, disasters may befall, but through it all a calm establishment knows that a brighter tomorrow will dawn. The public at large is far readier to believe television's most fanciful fare than it is to accept the "proofs" that the end of the age is at hand. *New Yorker* cartoonists, when all other ideas elude them, could always squeeze one more laugh out of the white-robed bearded zealot with his surly sign announcing that "The End is Nigh." Or when city news was light, the reporter could knock out one more story about the tent revivalist, hoarse and sweaty, demonstrating with science and slides that the Antichrist is here. And the tired historian could drag out his old notes to give the lecture that always amused: "Deadlines God Failed to Meet." Yesterday's fashions are comic costumes today.

The pessimistic expectation of the world's swift demise, when God's vials of wrath are poured over a helpless, writhing human-ity and when Christ in visible and triumphant form returns to the earth, is often called premillennialism. That is, Christ's return will precede that glorious thousand-year reign of peace and joy when God will wipe away every tear and death shall be no more (Revelation 21:4). This view of how the world ends — that is, with a bang — must be distinguished from a millennial expectation that sees the world as getting better and better until, behold, Christian truth and love reign everywhere and the kingdom of God, we discover, does indeed exist on earth. This view of history (often called postmillennialism), far from being ridiculed, is fully absorbed into America's blood-stream. "Westward the course of empire takes its way"; North America, the scene of God's fullest revelation of himself in his-tory; Zion built in Massachusetts or Cincinnati or Salt Lake City. Unfolding events will make it plain: America is the apple of God's eye. This, clearly, is no notion for ridicule; it is made for embrace.

Ridicule, then, is reserved for those dissenters who stubbornly

refuse to see that every day in every way we are getting better
and better. Those who sin against societal confidence, crying
"Repent! Prepare To Meet Thy God!", deserve only to be
mocked. The "end at hand" when the Gross National Product
keeps enlarging? when the average annual income keeps rising?
when the free world's weaponry keeps improving? Ridiculous.

In contrast, great numbers of nineteenth-century Americans
revealed an almost hypnotic fascination with prophecies of the
world's imminent end. That sometime soldier, deist, and
preacher, William Miller (1782–1849) of upstate New York,
attracted hearers from most major denominations as with scripture, charts, and persuasive ingenuity he demonstrated that
Christ would come in 1843. Since Christ literally fulfilled all
prophecies in his first coming (born of a virgin, wounded with
many stripes, etc.), it is perfectly reasonable to assume that his
Second Coming will be a literal fulfillment of all scripture.
When, for instance, we are told that he will descend "suddenly,
in the clouds, in like manner as he ascended," we have every
reason to believe that it will happen in just this way. When
we are told of the majesty of his coming, "on a great white
throne, with power and great glory and all his saints with him,"
then this is what we confidently expect.

In explicating the prophecies of the Book of Daniel and the
Revelation to John, William Miller indicated that Old and New
Testaments perfectly agree. One may interpret the words of one
author by the explanation offered centuries later in another land
and another tongue. "God in his wisdom has so interwoven the
several prophecies that the events foretold are not all told by
one prophet." This principle of interpreting scripture through
other scripture is joined with another rule of interpretation: one
must search for the metaphorical as well as the literal meaning
of all figures in the prophetic visions. For example, "fire" in
its metaphorical sense refers to the justice or judgments of God;
"fire has a cleansing quality, so will the justice or judgments
of God." In this manner, then, one can see the Bible as more

than "a great store-house full of all the precious commodities
[the] heart could desire, thrown in promiscuously." One must
study, examine, compare, weigh, bringing the full meaning out
of every word, every sentence, from every part of the Bible.
The result of such labor will "of necessity be correct." For "Truth
is one undeviating path that grows brighter and brighter the
more it is trodden; it needs no plausible arguments nor pompous
dress to make it more bright, for the more naked and simple
the fact, the stronger the truth appears."

The simple, naked fact was that Christ would come from
the clouds sometime between 21 March 1843 and that same
date one year later. Some ridiculed even then, not so much the
notion of a Second Coming as the precision with which it was
predicted. The error, if there is one, said Miller, will be mine;
"be the wrong on my head." But, if Miller were right, then
"Where will you be? No space then for repentance. No,
no — too late, too late; the harvest is over and past, the summer
is gone, the door is shut, and your soul is not saved." Given
those incalculable odds, many repented, and waited. When by
22 March 1844 Christ had not visibly returned, a recalculation
put the date in October, on the Day of Atonement. That time
also passed without supernatural manifestations. It was a sorrowful day. Yet, from the ashes of the Great Disappointment, new
life emerged. The Seventh-Day Adventists, as one of the
healthiest manifestations of that new life, continue to wait for
that final trump, for God's great consummation. "This Movement that began in a whisper," writes its leading apologist,
"will finish as an impelling Loud Cry, reverberating to the ends
of the earth."

A generation after Miller's predictions, Charles Taze Russell
gathered a small group together in Allegheny, Pennsylvania,
"to consider the Scriptures relative to the coming of Christ and
His Kingdom." These adventists, ultimately adopting the name
of Jehovah's Witnesses, saw the year 1914 as the critical juncture
in the history of the world: "Millions now living shall never

die!" In that year the "times of the Gentiles," during which
the gospel has been preached more or less in every nation, will
end; the "present evil world" will be no more. Satan will be
bound, his power overthrown, and the millennial age will begin.
In that sweet time, pain, sorrow, and death will disappear; all
who were lost because of the sin of Adam will be restored; knowledge and righteousness will cover the earth as waters cover the
sea. True, some passages of Scripture, "taken disconnectedly,"
appear to support those optimists who see the world as ever
improving and the church as the ultimate victor in converting
all the world. But viewing God's Word "as a whole," one can
only conclude that evil will continue to rage and Satan's fury
will spread until, at last, Christ comes to chastise and rule over
an unrepentant world. Satan then will be chained, his six-
thousand-year reign at an end, and the espoused virgin Church
will with joy become the Bride of Christ.

When the 1914 expectation failed to be manifest on earth,
it was reinterpreted as having been fulfilled in heaven. There
Christ established his kingdom in preparation for his yet-
to-be-established kingdom on earth. What happened in heaven
is further confirmation that "the end of this political, commer-
cial, religious world is near." God delayed so that there would
be time for a few more to repent. "Repent! Prepare to Meet
Thy God!" Only a little more time remains, the dawn is
breaking. "Already the early rays of its aurora are brightening
the faces of God-fearing persons who see the prophecies of the
Holy Bible coming true." The Bible "outrightly says" that the
political rulers of the earth are fighting against God's kingdom,
which is to come. The Book of Revelation speaks of seven kings,
and then notes an eighth who "goes to perdition" (17:10–11).
Now the seven kingdoms of this world have successively been
Egypt, Assyria, Babylon, Persia, Greece, Rome, "and the Anglo-
American World Power." The eighth king, the Eighth World
Power, is the United Nations, which "stands for world domina-
tion by man, not by God." It typifies man-made political systems

and ideologies, the perverse tendency of men to "prefer their own political sovereignty to the universal sovereignty of Jehovah God. To the question, Who owns the earth? they answer, We do!" So collision with God is inevitable, and the confrontation between Him and the nations is imminent. "Crash! comes the head-on collision! See there the United Nations organization! Will it be able to stand its ground and repel the divine onslaught? Divine prophecy says No!" God's war, namely Armageddon, "will end with Jehovah God and his military forces of heaven the only ones remaining on the field of battle, gloriously victorious. The issue of world domination will have been settled forever, in favor of Jehovah!" In that fateful hour, only those who place themselves on the side of Jehovah God will survive: therefore, endure the present reproach of men for the sake of the future and eternal favor of God.

In the view of the Witnesses, "religion" is what the consenting Establishment does. Only the faithful few, cast off from society, are the true followers of Jehovah. Millennialists saw themselves as possessors of a private truth not granted to society at large. Such rigid sectarianism only aggravated the ridicule already coming their way. But ridicule from without merely strengthened the confidence and redoubled the effort within. Seventh-Day Adventists built schools and colleges, established hospitals and sanitariums, sent out medical evangelists and medical supplies, aided the ill-fed and ill-clad, and grew from around thirty-five hundred members in 1860 to ten times that number a century later. Jehovah's Witnesses, repeatedly at odds with the law, despised by capitalist and Communist alike, built a publishing empire of astounding proportion, issued their own translation of the Bible, sent workers around the world, built "Kingdom Halls" in city and suburb, and grew from a few thousand in 1900 to one million two generations later. The eager anticipation of that impending Loud Cry did not terminate the large world of easy-going, mildly amused consenters; it did create and sustain small worlds of disciplined, dedicated, ridiculed dissenters.

America hosts other sinners against the American dream. A different type of apocalyptic prophecy focuses not so much on God's glorious victory as upon man's — and America's — foul treachery. These prophets of calamity see America as tragically off-center, both theologically and politically, misguided, deceived, conspired against at home and abroad. While Christ can set everything aright, of course, following his triumphant return, it is important meanwhile to identify the enemy and check the spread of satanic power. What distresses the religious right most of all are those who pose as Christians but are not really such, just as the political right is most agitated by those who pose as loyal Americans but are not really such. The Antichrist is a clever deceiver. Many are duped into believing that they are serving God when in fact they are giving the Devil cause to rejoice. Treachery and dupery must be exposed; the separation of the true believer from the false must be accomplished.

Billy James Hargis (b. 1925), ordained at the age of seventeen by the Rose Hill Christian Church of Texarkana, Texas, organized the Christian Crusade in 1947, establishing its head-quarters in Tulsa, Oklahoma. The purpose of the crusade's "educational ministry . . . is to safeguard and preserve the Conservative Christian ideals upon which America was founded." In order to execute this purpose, it is necessary "to oppose, militantly and aggressively, any person or organization whose words or actions endorse or parallel the philosophies of leftists, socialists, or communists, intentionally or otherwise." In expos-ing publicly any infiltration of these subversive influences into American life, the crusade automatically discharges its chief obligation: namely, "to defend the Gospel of Jesus Christ." One does his work here on earth below, as best he can, while waiting for the promised reinforcements from heaven above.

Like other millennial prophets, these crusaders see the Day of Doom as nigh. But Armageddon is not some vague struggle in the sky or the forces of evil some ethereal demonic force

involved in the process of creation. Godless communism is the
Evil; it is Satan incarnate. When it takes over America, the
Day of Doom is here, and this takeover is more imminent than
anyone thinks. No nuclear holocaust is necessary, nor is any
sneak invasion of Russian soldiers required: ". . . there are more
than enough people inside the country willing to hand" it over
without a protest or whimper. New York City has more Communists than Moscow; this country of ours requires "only another
shove or two" to push it over the precipice. How soon will
all this occur? Hargis does not present the elaborate charts of
William Miller or the involved scriptural interpretations of
Charles Taze Russell. He is more concerned to read the "signs
of the times" in political terms. One supporter suggested that
"America could go down before the Communist tide within
four years from March, 1959." In 1960, Hargis observed that
"Some of the nation's best informed and patriotic Christian-
American citizens believe that unless there is an awakening
among American people quickly . . . Communism will take
over the nation in five to ten years at the most." If these specific
dates pass without doom descending, it is of course only God's
forebearance, granting his children a little more time to turn
from Satan, to seek righteousness. "Repent! The End is Near!"

Whenever Armageddon is scheduled to arrive, one can hardly
deny that the powerful operation of Antichrist is manifest today.
We see his power so clearly among the Russians, Satan's chosen
people. "Only Satan could inspire in human beings complete
dedication to utter folly, unspeakable horrors, and total
untruth." Communism, the total lie, is the "great red dragon"
prophesied in the Book of Revelation; it is that "deceiver of
the whole world" who can be conquered only "by the blood
of the Lamb and by the word of their [the faithful's] testimony"
(Revelation 12). Satan, as always, appears in so many guises.
Americans, therefore, must be trained to recognize the Antichrist
in all his forms and modes, whether "liberalism, socialism, pro-
gressivism or modernism." Attempts are made to purvey commu-

nism as something "new and wonderful," but it is not new at all. Communism is "old and terrible," having its beginning in that first rebellion of Adam against the commandments of God.

Christian Crusaders share with other millennialists their Doomsday and their Devil. They differ, however, in their mode of salvation. For, in practical terms, they see salvation as owing more to the vigilance of men than to the intervention of God. America itself, "one of the greatest gifts that God has ever given men," can be the Determiner of history. America can first save herself and then proceed to save the world. What Americans must do above all is remember their heritage "as a Christian country, led by the Spirit of the Living God." Rightly understood, a crusade of Americanism is a crusade for Christianity, and vice versa. America, "the freest of free nations, the loveliest of all homelands, and the most wonderful country in world history," is God's elect nation. As such she has the responsibility to promote righteousness over all the earth, to "do battle in the name of the Lord Jesus Christ." To wage so heroic a battle, America must purify herself, must become ritually clean. She must cut away the morbid infection found in the Supreme Court, the deceitful press, the civil rights movement, the election process, the ranks of labor, the hosts of church members, and the Department of Health, Education, and Welfare. Communism infects every phase of American life; it is the solemn, sacred task of the Christian Crusade to expose the "sinister brotherhood," to root out the "slithering subversives." When that task is finally done, then the real citizens of America, "with the cross of Christ and the American Flag as our only standard," will march on to ultimate victory.

In a sense, therefore, these millennialists really oppose the millennium. Should God choose to stay His almighty hand, this is no Great Disappointment as it was for the Adventists but a Great Victory. The faith of other premillennialists is that Christ will descend "on a great white throne, with power and great glory and all his saints with him." The faith of the Christian

Crusaders is that men may seize the helm of history so that heaven can wait. Anti-communism is the only gospel and Nation the only God. Apostles of fear and agents of intimidation, the radical right is often itself an object of fear and deep·suspicion. In the 1950s particularly, the American public was engulfed in a paroxysm of fear as the freedom of dissent, the safety to dissent, plummeted. In a post-Peking, post-Moscow era of detente, reaction to the radical religious right shades from fear into fear's next-of-kin, ridicule. In the instabilities and uncertainties of military overruns and overkills, of political shifts and misalliances, the reaction, tomorrow, may be fear once more. "Repent! The End is Near!" Ridiculous?

The Patronized

Somewhere between good-humored toleration and casual indifference lies an attitude of superiority with which certain religious dissenters in America are greeted. These misfits it is not necessary to destroy though it may be wise to limit their numbers; nor need they be exiled, only excluded from a broad and easy participation in American life; finally, it is not even necessary to fear or to ridicule them since their power is restricted and their social standing is in question. They are, then, merely patronized, their visible ethnic diversity and religious peculiarity·being a welcome witness that America permits dissent, that Americans are persons of good will.

Except that the nation's treatment of the Oriental in the nineteenth century was not precisely a model of good will. West Coast economic hostility to Chinese labor together with a pervasive American assurance of Anglo-Saxon superiority brought about protests, demonstrations, and outrages in the 1860s and 1870s. These in turn led to the first formal limitation on immigration by the United States government: the Chinese Exclusion Act of 1882. Similar disdain for a "servile" and "immoral" immigrant population from Japan led to the nicely named

Gentleman's Agreement of 1907–08 that sharply reduced Japanese emigration. It also led to a California Alien Land Act in 1913 that effectively excluded the Japanese from owning agricultural land in that state. With the final immigration restrictions of 1924, America had been saved from the Yellow Peril; irrational fears of an alien race could be put to rest. They could be put to rest, that is, until in the aftermath of Pearl Harbor in 1941 an eruption of irrationality, panic, and greed caused some one hundred thousand Japanese Americans to be "relocated" from their homes, shops, and truck farms to the security of a barren and barbed-wire America farther east.

Upon coming to America, many Chinese and Japanese were converted to Christianity, though never in the numbers that early missionaries envisioned. For others the continuing allegiance to Buddhism or to Shinto, or to the mixture of the two, was evident in the temples and shrines rising along the West Coast. The force of Buddhism was more powerfully evident in Hawaii where the competition with Christianity was more evenly matched. In 1898 the first Young Men's Buddhist Association was established in San Francisco and seven years later the mainland's first Buddhist temple was dedicated there. The Buddhist Churches of America, incorporated in 1942, represents the True Jodo (or Jodo Shin) sect of Japanese Buddhism, the largest strain of "native" Buddhism in North America. Respectful attention was later give to Zen Buddhism and to its principal American center, Tassajara Hot Springs, one hundred and fifty miles south of San Francisco. Even an eclectic form of sectarian Shinto, the Church of Perfect Liberty, has established a headquarters in the United States, in Glendale, California. Oriental religion, transported to America as part of the "personal baggage" of the immigrant, attracted little attention. One could easily forget, or never know, that it was there.

The situation was altered, however, when the exotic flowering of the religious East began to win its share of converts. The World Parliament of Religions, assembled in Chicago in 1893, provided a major forum for the religions of the Orient. Opening doors and eyes to that largely unknown world, the parliament conveyed with special effectiveness the richly woven traditions of Buddhism and Hinduism. Occidental Americans for the first time learned in some detail of the varieties and differences within Buddhism itself. The vibrancy of northern or Mahayana Buddhism was amply revealed but also the ancient traditions preserved in Ceylon and the unique combinations of myth and rite in Tibet. From the vantage point of Buddhism alone the parliament was a splendid and impressive show. Unlike so many world congresses, however, it actually started significant new cultural trends.

One of the participants in that Chicago congregation, Soyen Shaku, returned to America in 1905 for a somewhat longer visit. His book, *Sermons of a Buddhist Abbott*, published in Chicago in 1906, served as the first extended introduction to Zen for a general American audience. In 1930 the first Zen Institute in America was established in New York under the direction of Sokei-an Sasaki. By far the foremost interpreter of Zen to Americans, however, was D. T. Suzuki (1870–1966), outstanding Buddhist scholar and superb apologist. Though a native of Japan, Suzuki lived in America from 1897 to 1909 and again from 1949 to 1957. His latter visit coincided with and strongly abetted the boom in Zen meditation, Zen puzzles, Zen artistry, exercises, and doctrine. The Oriental dissent from America's dominant religious pattern, it was soon evident, would no longer be confined to the immigrant. Out of the nation's midstream, writers, theologians, artists, and the young from all disciplines or none pursued Zen's un-American path. The distinguished Benedictine monk, Aelred Graham, published a volume in 1963 entitled *Zen Catholicism*; in 1969 Tibetan holy men opened a meditation center in San Francisco; and in 1971 William Johnston's *Christian Zen* appeared. The exotic was becoming domestic. As long as the numbers remained small, however, one could still safely condescend and cooly patronize.

With respect to Hinduism, the infusion into American culture
followed similar lines, except that no appreciable influx of Hindu
immigrants led the way. In a limited manner, New England's
Transcendentalists did lead the way on a literary-philosophical
level through their attention to the Upanishads. On the more
popular level, however, the Parliament of Religion again was
the breakthrough. Literally "in living color," representatives of
Hinduism presented their faith not as a decadent inheritance
collapsing before Christian missions but as an appealing,
resilient, self-reforming religion. Hinduism, Swami Vivekenanda
explained in Chicago, has survived all challenges and all heresies
from before the beginnings of recorded history. Each time it
has "receded only for a while, only to return in an all-absorbing
flood, a thousand times more vigorous" than before. Vedanta,
the name under which the Hindu mission to America was con-
ducted, is based on the ancient Vedas, he explained, but more
fundamentally it is based upon the spiritual truth that underlies
all Indian literature and, indeed, all religions of the world. In
their deepest nature, all men are divine. Vedanta intends to
assist men, East and West, in discovering and then manifesting
the Godhead that eternally dwells within them. All men are
more than mere brothers: all men are one. Drawing heavily on
the teachings of India's modern Hindu reformer, Sri Ramakrishna
(1836–1886), Vedanta did not seek great masses of converts;
rather, "it only seeks to clarify our thought, and thus help us
to a truer appreciation of our own religion and its ultimate aim."
Such a mild, quiet dissent.

Yet, Vedanta's "guest-teachers, not missionaries" did make
converts, did establish propaganda and recruiting centers across
America, did engage in theological dialogue and defense. The
1946 publication of Yogananda's *Autobiography of a Yogi* presented to public view a persuasive example of the blessings of
Hindu meditation and mysticism. The Self-Realization Fellowship, established two decades earlier in Los Angeles by
Yogananda, became a popular center itself even as it served as

the headquarters for meditation circles and churches in major cities of the United States and beyond. The conversions that have attracted greatest attention, however, came in the context of the counter-culture outbursts of the 1960s. A youth culture, rejecting a packaged and promoted "American way of life," often rejected a Judeo-Christian heritage that they — like others — identified as part of the same package. "Pop Zen," instant satori, magic mantras, and ten minutes of Yoga with the morning cereal were among the immediately visible results. A veritable tidal wave of publicity on behalf of the Maharishi Mahesh Yogi swept the country in 1968, suggesting that half of Hollywood and of hard rock fans everywhere had found the solution to life's puzzles in transcendental meditation. When the Maharishi left America to return to his ashram in India, the movement lost its most colorful advertisement.

Meanwhile, some communes displayed more serious and sustained efforts to comprehend and to embody the religious insights of the East. The Lama Foundation in the Sangre de Cristo mountains of northern New Mexico was one of the more disciplined efforts; begun in 1967, it also appeared to be one of the more durable and stable religious communes. Devotion to Yoga is also evident in the Ananda Cooperative Community in Nevada City, California, as well as in the Himalayan Academy that in 1962 settled in Virginia City, Nevada. In the latter commune, vows of celibacy and poverty are taken as a more monastic mode of self-realization is pursued. Most Americans, however, if they saw the new flowering of Eastern religion at all found it personified in the young followers of the Krishna Consciousness movement. With shaved heads, painted faces, saffron-robed bodies, these young dissenters extended their begging bowls to passersby as they chanted, "Hare Krishna! Hare Rama!" And passersby did not understand but smiled, patronizingly, and moved on.

As the great American symphony plays on, the dissonant notes of Hinduism and Buddhism will without question continue to be heard, for both religions have a vast literature, abundant philosophical and existential insights, and sharply alternative life styles. So to a lesser extent will the offbeats of Shinto and Islam be heard, lesser in Shinto's case because the literature is not vast or the existential alternatives so clear;* lesser in Islam's case because it travels a good way along the same theological road with Judaism and Christianity. The East intrigues even as it mystifies. Religiously it remains a social misfit for obvious historical reasons. In addition to theology, however, language, race, ethnicity, and nationalism also play some part. As they do for that large and largely invisible minority in the United States: the Mexican-American.

Of America's forty-five to fifty million Roman Catholics, approximately one-fourth are of Latin American descent. Yet, the largest concentration of Spanish-speaking peoples in the United States, the Mexican-Americans of the Southwest, protest that they have had a fair share in neither the bounty of their country nor the rule of their church. On both counts, they are correct. With respect to the country's bounty, the efforts of labor union leader and pious Catholic, Cesar Chavez, have begun to make a change. With regard to any "ecclesiastical reapportionment," the clouds of change are hardly larger than a man's hand. Mexican-American representation in the Catholic hierarchy and priesthood, rather than approaching an equitable 25 percent, actually amounts to about 1/10 of 1 percent.

History as well as inertia help account for this anomaly. The Mexican Revolution in 1912 not only alienated the church from the state but to a degree it also alienated the church from the people. Anticlericalism pervaded Mexico, this despite the leadership — and life — that Father Miguel Hidalgo gave to the 1810 War of Independence. (That Father Hidalgo, the learned and many-sided visionary hero of the Mexican Revolution, still stands under a ban of excommunication reflects

*Shinto's Church of Perfect Liberty, for example (see above, p. 121), is most visible in California for its attachment to and development of golf courses.

even as it perpetuates alienation between church and people.)
Prior to the revolution, moreover, the immigrants into the
Southwest stemmed chiefly from those classes and those geo-
graphic areas where the Roman Catholic church was regarded as
inseparably linked with aristocratic privilege and exploitation.
Further, the Church raised few clergymen up from the lower
agricultural classes. When the United States expanded into the
southwestern regions, this nation's Catholic authorities were
preoccupied with the heavy immigration of European Catholics
into Eastern cities. Those Eastern communities prospered and
grew healthy in the second half of the nineteenth century, while
the Southwest and especially the non-Anglo Southwest remained
neglected and poor. Native leadership was rare (most bishops
were French), parochial schools few, and Protestant proselytizing
vigorous. With the rest of the country busy meeting its
economic, educational, and religious challenges, the Southwest
was left to fend for itself.

As Anglo intrusions increased, the Spanish-speaking element
was also obliged to fight for cultural survival. Religious dissent
played a dramatic role in the waging of that battle. Whatever
the precise origins of the Penitentes, the Spanish brotherhood
in New Mexico attained its vigor and high visibility only in
the nineteenth century when a surrounding culture threatened
to swallow the Spanish-American minority. Two establishments
forced the dissenters into a secretive and determined opposition:
first, an Anglo-Protestantism that migrated in force into northern
New Mexico; and, second, a French Catholicism that asserted
its authority with intensified vigilance. Confronted with this
double invasion, *Los Hermanos Penitentes* clung even more desper-
ately to their unique ritual. That ritual, which took place each
year during Lent, intensifying in Holy Week itself, was characterized by a penance through flagellation and self-mortification.
"For the love of God," pain was inflicted and whippings (with
yucca or leather or wire) endured. In the re-creation of Christ's

Passion, heavy crosses were dragged on Good Friday to the appointed place of worship. To the accompaniment of hymns, liturgical readings, severe scourgings, the procession made its painful way. Ultimately, the *Christo*, already chosen, was tied — not nailed — to the cross and the ritual crucifixion took place.

Protestant missionaries, unfamiliar with even milder forms of penitential piety, were horrified by the extravagances of New Mexico's Penitentes. In disgust, they denounced the "barbarities" and ignorant superstitions of foreign fanatics. An American army surgeon, presumably forgetting an earlier Golgotha, asked: "What kind of a God is it who would accept such an atonement or approve of its offering? The faces of the participants were mostly of a brutal type . . ." The only thing good about the Penitentes ritual, from the Protestants' point of view, was that it clearly indicated the perversity if not the essence of Roman Catholicism. Thrown on the defensive, French Catholic bishops, as much outsiders as the Protestant missionaries, condemned the brotherhood and forbade it to continue its traditional pattern of penance. As early as 1833 ecclesiastical authorities attempted to bring the Penitentes into conformity with prevailing Catholic practice in America, but to no avail. Sterner language and sterner measures came half a century later when Archbishop Jean Baptiste Salpointe issued his second encyclical concerning these troublesome dissenters:

With regard to the Society called *Los Penitentes*, we firmly believe that it fully deserves all blame. Consequently, it must not be fostered. This society though perhaps legitimate and religious in its beginning so greatly degenerated many years ago that it has no longer fixed rules, but it is governed in everything according to the pleasure of the director of every locality; and in many cases it is nothing else but a political society.

Archbishop Salpointe therefore decreed that the sacraments be withheld until the Penitentes reform; when they failed to reform, excommunication followed in 1899. Two generations later the brotherhood still existed, though weakened both in numbers and in allegiance to older forms.

In the twentieth century, the voice of Spanish-speaking dissent was heard far from the hills of New Mexico. When prosperity finally did filter into the Southwest, the Mexican-American found himself filtered out of a proportionate share. The desperate working conditions of the farm laborers, the sordid hovels in which migrants lived, the subsistence on tortillas and coffee, the caste divisions between Anglo and Chicano, and — bitterest blow of all — the apparent indifference of the Church, these all filled America's second largest minority with despair, and some with resolve. As far as the chanceries and councils of the Church were concerned, the question was not merely one of numerical balance. It was more a matter of what Christian concerns were recognized and what concerns not even felt. Could the Church, for example, continue to hold itself aloof from hunger and deprivation? In the Los Angeles diocese where about one-half of the parishioners were Mexican-American, a 1937 editorial in the diocesan *Tidings* declared in those depression-darkened days: "Christ did not found the Church to be a mere humanitarian institution. The Church is a teacher. She works to bring God's grace to the souls of men. . . . She has, in fact, plenty to do to attend to her own business." A voice of condescension in the midst of suffering was unlikely to calm or weaken a religious dissent.

In 1943, the first Catholic conference ever to deal explicitly with the peculiar, pressing needs of the Mexican-American people was called together in San Antonio, Texas. A "Bishops' Committee for the Spanish-speaking," formed soon thereafter, directed Catholic energies and funds from purely pastoral concerns to matters of social justice. In California four priests were assigned in 1949 not to local parishes as tradition demanded but to migrant workers and their families wherever they temporarily "settled." These clergymen of the "Spanish Mission Band," made poignantly aware of the severe economic distress

among migrant workers, inevitably involved the Church in the
explosive issue of labor organization. Lines were drawn between
the Mexican-American community on the one hand and the
entire agricultural industry on the other. By the time the smoke
of that battle began to clear, the bracero program had been
terminated, lengthy strikes had been called, large landowners
had attacked the Church, and quantities of grapes and lettuce
sat unpurchased on supermarket shelves. One other result of
that confrontation was that by 1970 most Americans were prepared to admit that a Mexican-American minority did exist.
By that time, the Church was also prepared for such an admis-
sion.

For on 5 May 1970, in San Antonio, Patrick (Patricio) F.
Flores was elevated to the episcopate of the Roman Catholic
Church. Out of a hierarchy of two hundred and twenty-five,
one bishop was now Mexican-American. The ordination of
Bishop Flores was singular in other respects. Blending with the
Mexican Cinco de Mayo holiday, the "celebration" of the Mass
took on more than its usual meaning. A mariachi band rather
than a cathedral organ provided the music. An informal,
enthusiastic crowd, with *barrio* Chicanos side by side "with
plume-hatted and white-tie-and-tailed Knights of Columbus,"
burst into frequent applause. The epistle was read by Cesar
Chavez, while banners waved in tribute to him along with
Miguel Hidalgo, Emiliano Zapata, and "Juan XXIII." Audiences
in Mexico City, Los Angeles, and San Antonio, joined by television, could take some hope that a Church, if not a nation,
had started taking steps to remedy a century of neglect.

However uplifting the melodies of mariachi bands, they were
no substitute for sustained and organized vigilance. In the name
of "La Raza," the people, Mexican-Americans were asked to rally;
in the name of "Catolicos Por La Raza," Mexican-American
churchmen agitated for an ecclesiastical institution more
interested in serving the poor than in being served by them.
In 1969 a group of Mexican-American priests joined together

to enlarge the share of "the people" in the ministry and the consciousness of American Christendom. The resulting organizations, PADRES (in English, "Priests for Religious, Educational and Social Rights"), contended that only special ministries could meet the special needs of a widely scattered Mexican-American population. Hoping to correct Catholicism's Irish and German orientation even in areas where two-thirds of the Catholics were Mexican-American, these PADRES urged the establishment of a cultural center for the Hispanic Southwest. Some members of PADRES even argued that only a National Chicano Church could ever adequately represent or minister to La Raza.

More than a slogan, La Raza is of course a cause and a movement; it seeks social action along with ethnic pride and identification. Beginning in 1970, La Raza had another voice in *Aztlan: Chicano Journal of the Social Sciences and the Arts.* Published at the University of California, Los Angeles, *Aztlan* stands for a territorial as well as a cultural unity, these together creating a kind of religious mystique. The Southwest belongs to our people, "belongs to those who plant the seeds, water the fields, and gather the crops, and not to foreign Europeans." Pilgrims felt that way in claiming the lands of the Indians; Black Muslims felt that way in claiming the land of the white man. La Raza turned out to be plain Americans after all.

The Sentimentalized

> *Thoughts that great hearts once broke for, we*
> *Breathe cheaply in the common air.*

James Russell Lowell's words haunt the student of American religion. Brave battles when reviewed generations later become tame or insipid or possibly even embarrassing. Ancestral heroism is transmuted into quaintness and eccentricity. The gold of a dissent that hearts broke for reaches us in a debased coinage. We visit the Ephrata cloister, buy the Shaker furniture, listen to the Moravian melodies, smile at the whimsical spellings, wonder at the archaic fashions, ignore the tangled doctrines, and take comfort in our own emancipation. Dissenters are only the crotchets of history.

The Mennonite tradition illustrates how sentimentality softens the brutal past: the indiscriminate persecution and martyrdom of the sixteenth century, the somewhat more selective persecution and martyrdom of succeeding centuries. The radical left of the Continental Reformation, the Anabaptists, had the distinction of being despised by nearly everyone. To Calvinists and Lutherans, no less than to Roman Catholics, the radicals threatened the peace of society and the progress of Christianity. Resisting firmly every identification of the civil with the ecclesiastical realm, Anabaptists refused to bear arms, to take civil oaths, to support a state church, to see any merit in the baptism of infants too young to choose a faith they might have to die for. In Switzerland, where under Conrad Grebel the movement began in 1525, enormous energies were expanded to destroy this intolerable dissent. Execution by sword, by fire, and — since these rebaptizers liked water so much — by drowning took away hundreds, then thousands. After the beheading of Bishop Hans Landis in Bern in 1614, execution was set aside for gentler persuasion. For another two hundred years, until 1810, Switzerland's radical dissenters endured imprisonment, torture, loss of property, denial of civil rights, deportation, exile.

Meanwhile, radical reformers also appeared in Holland. Under the leadership of Menno Simons, Anabaptists recovered from the bitter associations with Münster and its wild apocalyptic expectations. They also somehow survived the loss from their ranks of the more than two thousand men, women, and children executed in the lowlands. Menno Simons, who served as bishop or elder in both Holland and northern Germany, provided through his writing a solid theological base and through his name the identification of the Anabaptist strain that managed to survive: the Mennonites.

From Switzerland and Holland, Mennonite families moved

either by choice or necessity into nearby areas of Germany, then to Austria and Prussia, then in bolder strides to North America and to Russia. Dutch Mennonites settled in Germantown, Pennsylvania, as early as 1683; larger numbers of Mennonites from the lower Rhine Valley arrived over the next two or three decades. In small communal knots Mennonites continued to come to the United States during the nineteenth century, sizable blocs fleeing Russia in the 1870s and again after World War I and II. The internal cohesion of each migrating fellowship was intimate and tight; nevertheless, among the several groups disagreements and ultimately factions arose. In the sixteenth century itself, Jacob Hutter, emphasizing the common ownership of property, welded together a group of Austrian Mennonites loyal to his special vision; long after he was burned at the stake in 1536, successive generations of Hutterites preserved and honored his name. In Switzerland toward the end of the seventeenth century, Jakob Ammann called for a stricter separation from lapsed or sinful members, and around this distinctive practice of "shunning" the Amish version of radical dissent arose.

From the canton of Bern, from nearby Alsace and the Palatinate, the Amish emigrated to America in the eighteenth and nineteenth centuries. Settling initially in Pennsylvania, notably in Lancaster County, the Amish moved later into the Midwest, concentrating in Ohio and Indiana. America's immigrants generally have found that "you can't go home again," but of the American Amish this is uniquely true, for no European Amish communities survive for them to return to. Sectarian separations that flourished in the expansiveness of an earlier America withered in the cramped quarters of Europe. The division, for example, between the Old Order Amish and the Mennonite Church in this country has no counterpart abroad. The Amish have either been absorbed into the main body of Mennonites or else have in ways and at times unknown lost their distinctive identity. Communes need land, and this America, unlike Europe, was able to provide. In a still largely rural America,

the Amish of a century ago were able to form self-sufficient,
homogenous communities, shunning not only the transgressor
in their midst but most of the world around them as well.

Gradually Americans at the edge of those self-contained
enclaves came to know something of these quiet, quaint dissenters: their beards, their preference for hooks and eyes over
buttons, their foot washing, their nonviolence, their agricultural
diligence and efficiency. As the world moved on, the Amish
declined to do so, with the result that the eccentricities became
more obvious and more the occasion of comment: no electricity,
no automobiles, no television, no welfare checks, no acceleration
of life in order to modernize and "improve" their standard of
living. If this is all there was to religious dissent, who could
complain? who could be anxious? If the Amish were misfits,
so what? A rococo society could use a bit of plainness now and
then. At least the Amish were safe and could be sentimentalized.
Or were they? Two possible exceptions to that comfortable conclusion gave one pause.

The first potential danger zone related to peace and war, subjects of some concern in all societies. Amish pacifism is part
of the consistent Mennonite testimony against war, a testimony
that goes back to Menno Simons and back, indeed, to the New
Testament. Menno wrote that "our weapons are not swords and
spears, but patience, silence and hope, and the Word of God.
With these we must maintain our cause and defend it." In the
light of the calamities then befalling all of Europe's Anabaptists,
he added that "true Christians know no vengeance, no matter
how they are mistreated." Through repeated persecution and
throughout Europe's protracted religious wars, the Mennonite
maintained his pacifist stance, winning the enmity of Protestant
and Catholic warriors alike. Partly to escape this incessant
militarism, Mennonites left Europe for countries that offered
exemption from military service — such as Russia — and to
countries that seemed safely removed from the European struggle — such as America.

The American Revolution, however, was a "people's war" from which residents could hardly hold themselves aloof. In Berks County, Pennsylvania, Amish were thrown in jail and even threatened with executions that never came off. When the Lancaster County Mennonites refused to form military associations for the defense of the area, they were subjected to growing abuse and mistreatment. A committee "of inspection and observation," meeting in 1775, urged that in the interests of harmony and union "so absolutely necessary in the present crisis in public affairs" Mennonites no longer be harassed by "violent and ill-disposed people." This toleration was especially fitting since these pacifists have been willing "to contribute cheerfully to the common cause otherwise than by taking up arms." Some of these cheerful givers, however, having fled Europe's frying pan only to fall into an American fire, left for a quieter, calmer Canada. In the wars of 1812 and 1848, only volunteers were called to fight so that pressure on these dissenters was minimal. The hard years of the Civil War again brought abuse, or flight, or fine; again, the pacifist communities of rural America indicated, as they had in 1775, that they could feed the hungry and give the thirsty to drink but beyond that they could not go. "We have dedicated ourselves to serve all Men in everything that can be helpful to the Preservation of Men's Lives, but we find no Freedom in giving, or doing, or assisting in any thing by which Men's Lives are destroyed or hurt."

In World War I the Mennonites found themselves accused of pro-German sympathies, of cowardice, and of violations of the Espionage Act because they discouraged their fellows from buying war bonds and contributing to war chests. Animosities against them were aggravated when many young men refused even to accept the government's definition of noncombatant service since such service still required the wearing of a military uniform and since such service so clearly contributed to the total war effort. Meeting near Goshen, Indiana, in 1917 the Mennonite General Conference hoped to make clear that their pacifism was neither treachery nor cowardice but obedience to a higher law and to a kingdom "not of this world."

As a Christian people we have always endeavored to support the government under which we lived in every capacity consistent with the teaching of the Gospel as we understand it, and will continue to do so; but according to this teaching we cannot participate in war in any form; that is, to aid or abet war, whether in a combatant or noncombatant capacity. We are conscious of what this attitude, under existing circumstances, may mean. No one who really understands our position will accuse us of either disloyalty or cowardice. . . .

Many, however, chose not to understand, covering homes, businesses, and church buildings with yellow paint as befitted "slackers" and Kaiser-lovers. In Jasper County, Missouri, patriots were at work delivering the following notices to Mennonites:

FIRST AND LAST WARNING
You have been reported to the ALL AMERICAN SQUAD as a person who has failed in your obligation.
YOUR COUNTRY IS AT WAR!
This committee does not tolerate SLACKERS. Do your full duty to your country NOW! Or get out of Jasper County or suffer the consequences.
ALL AMERICAN COMMITTEE STRONG ARM SQUAD

Across America the Amish and other Mennonites nonetheless disassociated themselves from that "by which Men's Lives are destroyed or hurt." In doing so, they confessed their readiness to endure the penalties and the pain, "trusting the Lord for guidance and protection." One hundred and thirty-eight young Mennonites were court-martialed and sent to prison during the brief period of American involvement in World War I.

In the longer period of World War II both the Mennonites and the federal government were better prepared to handle this potentially explosive form of dissent. The Conscription Act of 1940, written in consultation with the Historic Peace Churches, provided that all persons "who by reason of religious training and belief" were opposed to any form of military service should, if drafted, "be assigned to work of national importance under civilian direction." The civilian direction was of great significance to the Mennonites who found their presence in the military camps, under military orders, in military uniforms to be by its very nature a compromise of their witness. The new legislation resulted in the formation of the Civilian Public Service that assigned conscientious objectors to soil conservation agencies, to forestry and park services, to general and mental hospitals, and other public tasks. Of the total of approximately twelve thousand conscientious objectors engaged in these duties during World War II, more than a third were Mennonites. Their jobs were under government direction, but their living conditions and social affairs were under the direction and at the expense of the churches. And since the men received no pay, the churches also had to provide for personal needs and raise money for the support of dependents. These hardships notwithstanding, Mennonites were generally better treated during this World War than in earlier ones. In the 1950s, in the course of America's prolonged peacetime conscription, further improvements were made, permitting Mennonites for the first time to serve abroad in relief work and health services and allowing for wages to be paid at the rates prevailing in the several agencies or institutions. America's greater tolerance for conscientious objection received a severe testing, however, when during the protracted Vietnam struggle the rejection of all war was confused and confounded with a rejection of this war. Could one's conscience dictate a selective objection to war? And could one's scruples be based on grounds other than that of religion? As these questions troubled the nation's courts, councils, and draft boards, a dogmatic and unrelenting pacifism revealed once more the capacity to alarm all-American squads symbolic of a militarism that increasingly penetrated every layer and every corner of contemporary life.

The second danger zone was education. In America the public school, viewed as the principal instrument of Americanization and assimilation, has enjoyed, as Sidney Mead noted, something of the status of an established church. To refuse to attend a public school is to raise immediate suspicions regarding one's Americanism. These suspicions can be largely allayed, however, if the private school will look as much like a public school as possible. On this score the Amish also failed. Where they built their own private schools, they were so unmistakably, defiantly Amish. Where there were no private schools, participation in the public schools was carping or reluctant or, above the eighth-grade level, simply absent. In Ohio and Pennsylvania, in Iowa and Wisconsin, sentimentality yielded to frustration, anger, and hostility in the confrontation between convention and dissent. Suddenly, the Amish were more than black buggies and beards: they were a menace to the state and even to themselves.

If education is an agent of assimilation (the state's point of view), it is also an agent for cultural transmission (the Amish family's point of view). When the culture to which one is being assimilated is similar to the one that a family wishes to have transmitted, conflict is small. In the case of the Amish, obviously, the life styles of Establishment and of Dissent were far apart. In Pennsylvania, the conflict was gradually resolved in the 1950s through a series of compromises that permitted the dignity of both sides to be preserved. Pennsylvania's school laws required attendance of all children, ages eight through seventeen, in a school where subjects prescribed by the State Board of Education were taught in the English language. Amish elementary schools were defined as parochial schools and the teachers agreed to work toward accreditation. Secondary education was defined in terms of the vocational training provided on the farm and in the home, so the thorny question of compulsory high school attendance was neatly avoided. In Ohio at the end of the 1950s, the State Department of Education determined that all twenty-two Amish elementary schools failed to meet state standards. In rendering their judgment on Amish deficiencies, the voice of a bureaucratic and impersonal Establishment was heard. Amish schools did not provide proper facilities for heat, light, ventilation, and sanitation; teacher aids were insufficient, while plans for "staff growth" were inadequate; playground equipment was not all that it should be and academic deficiencies were numerous. In Iowa during the 1960s state authorities, discovering similar shortcomings in Amish schools, ruled that, according to the stipulations of Section 299.8 of the Iowa Code, the children attending these substandard schools were in fact truants. In a remarkable show of force, the state moved into an Amish school with buses ready to transport the children to a proper school. Some of the young rebels ran out of the schoolhouse, crawled through a fence, and escaped through a cornfield. Others, protesting and weeping, were dragged to their buses as fathers prayed and mothers sobbed. Clearly, no time for sentiment.

The climax came in Wisconsin in 1972, or rather it came in Washington, D.C., when the Supreme Court (*Wisconsin* v. *Yoder*) decided what should be done to Amish children who refused to obey Wisconsin's compulsory school attendance law. The court's task was to balance the claims of the state against those of the parent and the commune-church, the claims of a modern majority against a tradition-directed minority, the claims of what the court called the "mainstream" against those of dissent. A "State's interest in universal education, however highly we rank it, is not totally free from a balancing process when it impinges on other fundamental rights and interests, such as those specifically protected by the Free Exercise Clause of the First Amendment and the traditional interest of parents with respect to the religious upbringing of their children. . . ." The balance had to be struck with respect to fourteen-and fifteen-year-old Amish children who had finished the eighth grade and whose parents refused to send them on to high school. Wisconsin's law required school attendance through a young person's sixteenth year.

The court indicated that dissent per se was not the issue,

for often the greater values of a civilization have been preserved by the religiously different, by those "who isolated themselves against all worldly influences against great obstacles." A way of life is not necessarily wrong merely because it "is odd or even erratic." On the other hand, in an age when dissent is so widespread, when radicals and hippies, "progressive" schools and "free" universities, abound, the legitimate interests of the state may be threatened. Great numbers may claim the right to establish schools of which the state does not approve, or they may even abandon schooling altogether. The gate to social disintegration and educational chaos cannot be opened so wide.

The decision, therefore, was to open it just a little — wide enough to render a decision favorable to the Amish, but no wider. Because the Amish have a long and continuous history "as an identifiable religious sect," because they are self-sufficient and no burden to society (no welfare checks or food stamps among the Amish), because they "have convincingly demonstrated the sincerity of their religious beliefs" and the vital connection between those beliefs and their mode of life, and because they provide a clear alternative method of education on the farm and in the home — because of all this the school authorities in this single case are wrong and the Amish are right. In its unanimously favorable opinion, the court was determined to limit the effects of its decision to this one group of religious dissenters. And that decision was made easier — perhaps it was made possible — by the fact that these dissenters were so few: between two and three hundred school children in the entire state of Wisconsin, fewer than twenty-five thousand Amish, old and young, in the entire United States of America. Whether dissent is sentimentalized, patronized, exiled, or destroyed is often determined by a count.

According to the figures perceived by mainstream America, it was safe to sentimentalize and indulge the Amish. It was even possible to exalt them on Broadway. In "Plain and Fancy," which opened in New York in January 1955, theatregoers could participate in the simplicity and charm of young love among the Amish. Life was tranquil and bucolic and abundant, as the concluding chorus revealed:

> *Sweet land of meadows golden*
> *And fat red barns for holdin'*
> *What goes to town on market day,*
> *Plenty of anything — plenty of everything*
> *In Pennsylvan-i-ay!*

A second musical comedy, "By Hex," opened in New York the following year; less successful than "Plain and Fancy," it closed in a few weeks, suggesting that sentiment may not be enough, even as entertainment.

The American experiment in religious freedom, falteringly begun at several points in the colonial era, more ambitiously launched with the First Amendment in 1791, is one of the bolder chapters in the American story. Often over the course of these centuries, the religious boldness has been more than a match for the political determination that, in matters of the soul at least, men shall be free. Dissent stiffened by religious vision and the certitudes of faith became society's severest critic and judge. More recently, religious dissent has seemed domesticated and tamed in comparison with the bitter outbursts of political dissent. Or the two have been in such close conjunction as to obscure the nature of motivation for the dissent. In the 1970s society's misfits abound, but what is their faith?

In the Amish school decision a hint is dropped that religion's possibilities for dissent may be widened in the days ahead, rather than sharply limited by inertia or by law. While the Supreme Court interpreted its Amish decision narrowly, Justice William O. Douglas in a partial dissent interpreted it broadly. He gave it a breadth not accepted by the court or yet perceived by the nation's saints. In its previous historic decisions, Douglas noted, such as those pertaining to the Mormons and polygamy, the court had decreed that antisocial activity "could be punished even though it was grounded on deeply held and sincere religious convictions. What we do today, at least in this respect, opens the way to give organized religion a broader base than it has ever enjoyed; and it even promises that in time Reynolds [the polygamy case] will be overruled." Should that come about, religious dissent may again place the severest strain upon the fabric of American society. The heartiest sinners against society will be once more its truest believers.

5

Epilogue:
New Directions
in Religious
Dissent

Religious dissent in America has, as we have seen, a rich past. That it is also a checkered past is but the nature of dissent. Schismatics, heretics, and misfits from the seventeenth century to the twentieth have at least taught us that religious dissent is 1) tough on bishops, and all other entrenched exercisers of ecclesiastical authority; 2) hard on creeds and all other dogmatically defined or uncritically assumed, proposition-packaged truth; and, 3) in constant tension with mainstream U.S.A., sometimes trying to alter the direction of the majority, other times asking only that society leave it alone. Churches, orthodoxies, and society's idols have sometimes bowed to or even been changed by the shrill voices of dissent; more often, the pachyderms of consent have lumbered on their appointed rounds. Or, a committee — more recently a presidential commission — has been appointed.

A dissent that could not "lick them" often joined them. The pattern of the small and purified elite, withdrawn from established religion and disdainful of a compromised and acquisitive society, itself becoming part of that establishment and social order is too familiar to require elaboration. Nothing fails like success. It is after all far more comfortable to move within the warm and well-lardered home than it is to stand outside shaking one's fist at the frosty panes. Within the home, moreover, one has a far better opportunity to influence, perhaps take over, the

management. Dissenters standing outside of society brighten history more often than they change it — or at least this is sufficient
rationalization for coming in out of the cold. Other dissenters
that could not "lick them" sternly declined to join them; their
graves litter the byways of history. Even their demise, however,
sometimes testified to their success; the facet of truth that had
been their vision was quietly and without thanks absorbed into
the myth or ritual or life style of the winning team. Yet others
died because what seemed a vision of truth turned out to be
only the "friar's lantern," a foolish fire.

   In the American past, both in the successes and failures of
religious dissent, in its verities and its follies, one finds roots,
or at least analogues, for many of the contemporary sins against
love, against faith, against society. Current concerns for social
justice have their counterparts in the conscientious dissent of
a Reinhold Niebuhr or a Dorothy Day. The pride of race long
ago provided the momentum for a powerful restructuring of
ecclesiastical institutions. Isaac Backus knew what it meant to
"do one's own thing" in the name of authentic, immediate
experience. Reactions against sterile reason and dehumanization
moved Orestes Brownson, Margaret Fuller, and Theodore Parker
to put forward a contrasting world view. O'Kelly Methodists
understood and rejected the phobias regarding "law and order,"
while Cumberland Presbyterians foresaw that too much emphasis
could be placed upon the academic experts and the gospel of
salvation by transcript. Today's call for a new sense of community
is anticipated in the schism of the Poles, the exodus of the Mormons, the tenacity of the Amish. And the notion that tomorrow's
world can be better, must be better, than today's is the driving
force in almost all of the dissenters whom we have surveyed.

   None of this is intended to suggest that the contemporary
world is without novelty. Today's scene and the varied ways
of "making it" reek with novelty. All the bubbling unrest and
social experimentation suggest, in fact, that dissent is omnipres-
ent. Yet novelty is not the equivalent of dissent: though fashions

in clothing are novel, they are at the same time among the strangest outcroppings of the mountainous establishment. Nor is dissent to be treated as a synonym for every maladjustment, every therapeutic need, every instance of offensive taste, every aimless wandering over the earth, every display of pique, or every ill-humored tantrum. In a time of total instability any change can appear to be a dissent, whereas it may be only a mindless digression; it may even be an effort to put some of the broken pieces of consent back together. Dissent requires discipline and direction even to be dissent; to be historically significant dissent, it requires such other items as organization, program, continuity, timeliness, and luck.

Not all dissent, of course, is religious in its inspiration or its end. Religious overtones and undertones nonetheless often can be detected in dissent that is essentially political or sociological or psychological. In the 1967 march on the Pentagon, student activists and New Left radicals were joined by "witches, warlocks, holymen, seers, prophets, mystics, saints, sorcerers, shamans, troubadours, minstrels, bards, roadmen and madmen"— hardly a model of purely political protest. Civil rights marches and demonstrations have long revealed a pronounced religious flavor, the religious dissenters often being most critical of the careless indifference or cautious reform in their own establishment churches. Such formal structures as the "Clergy and Laity Concerned About Vietnam" even more clearly bring religious dissent into active partnership with political dissent.

In 1967 a Protestant, a Jewish, and a Catholic spokesman appealed to the institutions of religion to take action regarding *Vietnam: Crisis of Conscience.* The specific issue, though profoundly moral, is patently political in the sense that an effort is being made to change public policy. Even their language, the authors (Robert McAfee Brown, Abraham Joshua Heschel, Michael Novak) note, is more political than "religious"; nevertheless, "any discussion of how men live and die is a theological, moral and religious discussion, regardless of phraseology." Churches

and synagogues need to recognize the religious dimension of
foreign policy and then recognize their religious obligation with
respect to it. That obligation, in time of war, is to reconcile
men and nations, meaning at least to keep lines of communication open among nations and between the opposing factions
within a nation. Religion is not, as Thomas Jefferson once wrote,
an affair solely between man and his God: it is between man,
God, and the neighbor. Looking after the neighbor, if not quite
managing to love him, inevitably involves one in all the ramifica-
tions of foreign policy and domestic policy as well. Religious
institutions, even the largest and most respectable among them,
have the obligation not only to encourage conscientious expression of opinion by their members but the further obligation
"to support them when such speaking involves dissent from government policy. The ultimate loyalty of Christian and Jew is
not to government but to God." Finally, the authors plead with
organized religion to speak with its corporate voice for it has
a heavy responsibility, too long neglected, to sensitize the conscience of the nation and to help it move in a new direction.
Churches and synagogues must themselves repent in order to
lead a whole nation to repentance. These three lonely voices
of religious dissent, seeking an alliance with political dissent,
hoped to arouse consenters in both church and state in order
to turn a national policy around. The pachyderms lumbered on.

Sociological and psychological dissent is best represented in
contemporary America by its youth. A whole literature has
recently come into being explaining the young to the old, the
old to the young, the young to themselves, and the young to
all the world. The phenomenon of the "revolt of the young"
is neither uniquely American nor narrowly religious. But
religion, both in its older indigenous forms and in its novel
exotic manifestations, is so much in evidence within the youth
scene that it cannot be ignored. In the drug culture the expand-
ing of the mind becomes a quick trip through all the stations
of the cross, directly to the beatific vision. In a modernized

version of the familiar refrain, "and malt does more than Milton can to justify God's ways to man," pharmacology supersedes theology. Through alchemy, LSD is changed into a League for Spiritual Discovery. Through mescalin or psilocybin the doors to perception are opened, the beyond is found within, the paths to ecstasy are made plain. Unlike the Native American Church, most of these youthful pilgrims experiment outside of any religious tradition, apart from any cultic direction, and in a welter of confusion between the means employed and the end in view. "The Counterfeit Infinity," in Theodore Roszak's phrase, is more often a lure to destruction than, of itself, a vehicle of religious dissent.

In the fascination with the occult, with astrology and with magic, one sees both a rejection of religion and an approach to it. The religion that is rejected is that which has permitted itself to become overrationalized and oversecularized. When sacred time and sacred place are distinct from no other time and no other place, their power to attract and to transform is gone. Ezekiel recognized some time ago, as much modern religion does not, the necessity of separation between the holy and the common, the sacred and profane. Religion that the head finds wholly agreeable the heart finds emotionally sterile. Western religion, having over many generations accommodated itself to scholasticism, to the Enlightenment, to the demands of the scientific method, and to the positivistic temper, has won an intellectual respectability — and little else. In rejecting all that, the cult and occult fanciers have turned hungrily to another kind of religion — to the Jack Kerouacs, then the Alan Wattses and the Allen Ginsbergs, still later to the tantras, the sutras, the I Ching, to all the eroticism and mysticism and immaterialism of the Orient. A world view that had not made a long series of concessions to modern technology and profane secularity proved to be, not repugnant to the emanicipated young, but alluring and even nourishing.

Kenneth Keniston distinguishes between two types of youthful

dissenters: one is withdrawn, culturally alienated, and pessimistic, often finding his only surcease in the drug culture so
that his dropping-out is of one piece with his turning-on. The
other type of dissenter is politically active, optimistic, engaged
in protest and demonstration to rectify the wrongs of a value
structure that is basically sound. Without any sustaining
ideology of his own, the activist seeks short-term amelioration
of immediate problems. In keeping with the prevailing Western
pattern, his radicalism is likely nonreligious, possibly
antireligious. The young person whose dissent is grounded in
religious commitments may form still another type. If his loyalty
is to Zen, for example, he is alienated from his verbose and
technical Western order, but he may become an active apologist
for a new world view that gives dignity and meaning to his
life. If the dissenter's loyalty is to an underground, anti-
institutional, ecstatic Christian sect, he may then withdraw from
all political participation, being essentially pessimistic or indifferent with respect to man's capacities and society's progress.
In still other instances, youthful religious activity, however vigorous and however photogenic, may not be dissent at all. "Explo
72," gathering eighty thousand in Dallas's Cotton Bowl in the
early summer of 1972, was clearly religious and clearly youthful;
less clear was its dissent from established institutions, established
ideologies, or established cultural patterns and expectations. Of
the "Children of God" and other neofundamentalist sects of the
Jesus movement, or of the Reverend Arthur Blessit and his "Turn
on to Jesus" stickers along Los Angeles's Sunset Strip, one writes
with even less assurance concerning the nature or degree of their
dissent.

Dissent cannot therefore be equated with every flash of novelty
or with every departure from current fashion, even when these
are found in or near the houses of God. At the same time,
one cannot so narrow the definition of religious dissent as to
give it a single thrust, a consistent program, or even a certain
quality of result. To make of religious dissent some new kind

of orthodoxy that tomorrow will prevail would be perverse in the extreme. Dissent does not travel the well-paved roads but hacks its own trails through unfamiliar country. One cannot know in advance where the trails will go, or how far down them anyone will manage to get. One can be virtually certain, however, that all trails will not lead in the same direction. Religious dissenters of the "right" oppose and perhaps even cancel out the dissenters of the "left," whether those vague labels be applied to institutions or to orthodoxies or to the social and political order. The "new directions" of dissent, like its old directions, are many and contrary; remarkably, dissent is not thereby reduced to a nullity.

Rather, at a time when "religion is losing its influence," according to the responses that Gallup gathers, religious dissent may well gain in impact. Establishment religion's "lost influence" is in fact dissent's open invitation. If the traditional religious fare has become bland and weak, the problem may be less with religion and more with its professional hucksters. Religious dissent can more easily be heard when the thunderous pronouncements of once-powerful pulpits come forth in whispers. Religious dissent may also have more opportunity for expression when political dissent is so soundly squelched. Civil rights workers murdered in Mississippi, Black Panthers shot in Chicago, students killed at Kent State, twelve thousand arrested in May Day demonstrations in 1971: these unhappy events together with the monotonous familiarity of tear-gassing, wire-tapping, and head-knocking suggest the heavier liabilities of political dissent. Many doors open, therefore, to religious dissent; through which ones will it walk?

Against *Religion and the New Majority* by L. D. Streiker and G. S. Strober (1972), notwithstanding the theology of the *White House Sermons* edited by Ben Hibbs (1972), uninterested in the answer to D. M. Kelley's *Why Conservative Churches are Growing* (1972), religious dissent, at its most fruitful, will respond to those human needs not being adequately met. Human needs

do not radically alter, but the capacity or readiness of agencies
to meet those needs differs from one generation to another and
from one culture to another. Society as it moves in pendulum-
like fashion from one over-correction to another displays a great
gift for just missing the truth. When a vision of truth is perceived
and announced, it then is codified and institutionalized and dis-
torted. In its panting, heavy-footed pursuit of that vision, society's motto is "Everything to excess." The role of dissent is
to move a culture or a church or a university or a system back
from its hardened, formula-bound, unseeing and unfeeling
extreme toward the center once more. After years of petition
and pain, the move slowly begins, the momentum picks up,
and the center is again overshot. In the moving, not in the
positioning at either end of the swing, humanity — and possibly
epistemology — is best served. Against the deficiencies and
rigidities of a given time and a given place, religious dissent
rails. Those deficiencies determine the new directions. If animals
have a body wisdom that directs them in correcting dietary
deficiencies, perhaps humans have a soul wisdom that reveals
where essential spiritual nourishment can be found.

In the America of the 1970s, three new directions for religious
dissent appear likely to move that heavy pendulum. Dissenters
opt for mystery, seek community, and embrace joy. And in
each of these three paths, there is a high road and a low.

In preferring mystery over a clinical rationality, contemporary
religious dissent rejects both a theology that has become remote
and lifeless and an ecclesiasticism that has become impersonal
and "correct." Such a dissent also rejects the scientism of a John
Wesley Powell scandalized by the "hashish of mystery." A cultural elite in hot pursuit of impartial and impersonal objectivity
fails to attain that perfect objectivity but succeeds far too well
in fostering a demeaning impersonality. The baleful result is
a system that frets more about mutilating punch cards than
mutilating people; the cult of objectivity leads to research designs
that permit "control groups" to go without proper medication

or education in order that data might be gathered that will lead to "further investigation." Reason's ruling priesthood "mystify the popular mind by creating illusions of omnipotence and omniscience — in much the same way that the pharaohs and priesthood of ancient Egypt used their monopoly of the calendar to command the awed docility of ignorant subjects." Roszak, whose words these are, adds that our language has today become so debased and rhetoric so depersonalized that we manage to soften or hide hideous realities from ourselves, doing so by means of phrases that are remarkably technical or analytical or rational — or empty.

From all of this routinizing, sanitizing, and objective ordering of life, including the religious life, today's dissenter turns away. He turns to the Hasidic mysteries of a Jewish tradition, to the ways of knowing that mystics in the Christian tradition have honored and embodied. He turns to ancient prophecies and to modern prophets, even being willing to join with Tertullian once more in embracing that which is absurd. Most dramatically, he turns to the defiantly irrational Orient, forming a Himalayan Academy in Nevada or an Ananda Cooperative Community in California where Yoga and Self-Realization become the avenues of dissent. Or in the Sangre de Cristo mountains of northern New Mexico, he joins the twenty-five earnest souls in the Lama Foundation in a nonrational, eclectic search into the more mysterious realms of philosophy and religion.

This deliberate acceptance of mystery leads, along its high road, to humility: man does not and will not know all, man cannot and need not control all. That high road also leads to the humane, to the needs of the person more than the dictates of the machine. Against all the engineers of human consent, against the panderers of material progress and insatiable acquisitiveness, this new direction of dissent honors man as a member of the kingdom of ends, never of means only. But to choose mystery is to risk finding oneself on the low road. There the dissenter gets lost in the cult of the absurd, regarding incense as a substitute for insight, strobe lights as a surrogate for the beatific vision. Or, in an ultimate betrayal, those along the low road accept the establishment slogan that better living really is only a matter of better chemistry.

The search for community is as poignant a quest as can be found on the contemporary American scene. A "Nation of Strangers" says touch me, notice me, love me, need me. In the midst of our technocratic urban sprawl, the ancient biblical question, "Who is thy neighbor?" would receive the sincerest reply, "I haven't the faintest idea." Indifference turns to hostility, and unawareness becomes contempt. The church goes underground so that it can know and speak to and perhaps touch the neighbor, so that some sense of community can be regained. The hundreds of sensitivity and encounter groups across the continent, whatever else they say, testify that bureaucracies, power structures, and status-seekers offer very little community at all — whether within the churches or in society at large. Life is lonely. In an effort to escape a sentence to solitary confinement, men and women turn to the lodge, the club, the coven, brotherhoods and sisterhoods, the ethnic association, the veterans of, the class of, the natives of, the sons or daughters of, the arrangement, the affair, the group, and in utter desperation even to the piano bar of the jumbo jets.

Many turn to the religious commune, persons young and old, orthodox and heterodox, conservative and liberal. Near Americus, Georgia, Clarence Jordan in 1942 founded an interracial, self-sufficient Christian fellowship called Koinonia. Thirty years of scorn, economic boycott, and Ku Klux Klan vigilantism have not yet managed to destroy that communal bond. In the 1950s, young Mennonites established the Reba Place Fellowship in Chicago, deliberately choosing an urban setting where the commune would not turn in upon itself but would reach outward to feed the hungry, assist the poor, teach the retarded, and help the emotionally disturbed. In the 1960s and 1970s, young Jews gathered in Chabad Houses, and isolated Catholics turned from the world to monastic retreats just when monks and nuns had decided to give up the communal life to rejoin the world. Less traditional expressions of common faith were found in the Messiah's World Crusade (Larkspur, California), the City of Light (near Sante Fe, New Mexico), the Morning Star Faith: Thy Open Land Church (Sonoma County, California and near Taos, New Mexico), and the Brotherhood of the Spirit (Warwick, Massachusetts). The thirst for community, "the wish to live in trust and fraternal cooperation with one's fellows in a total and visible collective entity," has rarely been so plaintively in evidence. Since this desire is, in Philip Slater's words, "uniquely frustrated by American culture," only dissent makes genuine community possible, only dissent transforms equality from a slogan into an experience.

In this turn from loneliness, alienation, and competition toward cooperation and the ties that bind, some take the high road. They manage to demonstrate that in Christ, for example, there really is no East or West, slave or free, Gentile or Jew, female or male. The divine capacity for loving the sinner though not his sin becomes, here and there, a human capacity too; "acceptance" is not the text for a mild homily but a description of a simple, selfless way of life. Along the low road, in contrast, the passion for community becomes a mutual evasion of all responsibility, as the commune itself degenerates into a haven for the undisciplined and bored, the paranoid and amoral. Sensitivity groups, through mere amateurishness or sheer quackery, descend from a level of rescue and redemption to one of abandonment and exploitation. Community is lost and perhaps one's soul as well.

Finally, in their hearty embrace of joy, today's religious dissenters stand apart from most of America's earlier sinners against love or faith or society. The former engage not in painful schism, nor indulge in ponderous heresy, nor suffer lonely exile. It is time for a new song; it is perhaps a time, in E. B. White's phrase, not to save the world but to savor it. With the lightest

possible touch, one places a flower in the barrel of the establishment's gun, even though the gun is pointed straight at the
dissenter's heart. Or one dances in the protest march, changing
it from an angry confrontation to a happy parade, with balloons
and candy and streetside theater for all. If religion is a beautiful
instrument, then play it; do not use it as a terrestrial weapon
or as a celestial threat.

The musical *Godspell* primarily sets a tone, and that tone is
joy. From the initial "Prepare Ye the Way of the Lord" through
the bread and wine communion with the audience to the exuber-
ant post-crucifixion dancing, it is a joyful noise unto the Lord.
Such festivity, Harvey Cox points out, is not to be confused
with superficiality for a truly joyful religion recognizes tragedy
and squarely faces evil. Only an "antiseptic religion shies away
from guilt and terror as well as eros and mirth." Nor is festivity
the same as frivolity, for while the latter despairs of life, the
former is a celebration of it. In laughter there is both affirmation
and hope. Christ is a clown, "defeated, tricked, humiliated,
and tromped upon . . . infinitely vulnerable, but never finally
defeated." Faith has its playful dimension, as Black Protestants,
Mediterranean Catholics, and Hasidic Jews have never forgotten,
and as today's dissenters discover. They recall that "ecstasy" is
the traditional word for the nearest union with God and that
liturgy and prayer, like play, lift us from leaden legalism and
stultifying routine to other regions of awareness and élan.

On its higher path, the embrace of joy returns religion to
its prior and primitive role as a celebration of life. One dances
before the Lord with Davidic abandon; one sings heavenly praises
with exultation; one speaks in the flush of immediate inspiration;
one joins with Joyce's Molly and with Kazantzakis's Zorba in
shouting a lusty "Yes!" to life. A task performed "religiously"
is one done not with grim and methodical determination but
with laughter and good cheer. On its lower path, religion as
joy offers nothing to the soul, catering to and satisfying only
the appetites of the body. Gratification replaces gratitude, child-

ishness is mistaken for childlikeness, and sensuality becomes
a bondage instead of a release. Getting rid of "Puritan hang-ups"
serves as the threadbare excuse for every indulgence, every glut-
tony, every rape of the spirit, every manipulation or dismissal
of the neighbor. One walking the low road claims that he sees
most by staring at the sun.

Each new direction, therefore, has its perils no less than its
promises. Even if all dissenters took the high road, they would
not bring about a "return to religion" or a "revival of religion"
as these phrases are generally understood. It is the re-creation
of religion to which they are dedicated, in which both the wine
and the wine bottles are new. This is a high-risk undertaking.
For many modern sinners the wine will sour as community yields
to anarchy, as mystery equals muddleheadedness, as joy turns
to joyless pursuit. In the first century, amidst a plethora of fresh
dissent, the sober counsel was "Test everything; hold fast what
is good." It is sober counsel for every century, and every
generation. Dissent neither conducts the examination nor controls the results: it only insures throughout history that testing
will take place.

Important Dates

1492   Jews expelled from Spain

1549   British Parliament passes Act of Uniformity

1620   Dissenting separatists arrive in Plymouth, Massachusetts

1634   Disestablished Roman Catholics from Britain reach the shores of Maryland

1636   An exiled Roger Williams purchases land from the Indians and founds the settlement of Providence

1642   Virginia disfranchises Roman Catholics

1649   Maryland passes act of toleration (for Christians); Puritans flee Virginia for refuge in Maryland

1654   Jews arrive in New Amsterdam, and effort to eject them fails

1658   All Quakers banished from Virginia

1659   Two Quakers hanged in Boston

1680   Popé leads successful Indian revolt against Spain in Sante Fe, New Mexico

1682   Pennsylvania opens doors to religious dissenters

1683   Mennonites settle in Germantown, Pennsylvania; New York Assembly enacts toleration law limited to Christians

1689   British sovereigns William and Mary announce Act of Toleration

1707   Presbyterian Francis Makemie arrested and tried in New York

1708   Palatinate refugees begin to settle in Hudson and Mohawk River valleys; Connecticut passes Toleration Act

1725   Publication of Benjamin Franklin's youthful indiscretion, *A Dissertation on Liberty and Necessity*

1732   Fleeing Austrian persecution, the "Salzburger" Lutherans
        arrive in Georgia

1741–42 New England's Great Awakening, resulting in scores of
        schisms

1748   Isaac Backus forms New Light Church in Norwich,
        Connecticut

1752   Solomon Paine publishes his *Short View*, justifying the
        visible dissent from Connecticut's established churches

1767   Thomas Chandler in his *Appeal* argues for Church of
        England bishops to reside in America

1769   Society of Dissenters formed in New York to resist the
        exercise of episcopal powers in the British colonies

1773   Isaac Backus publishes his *Appeal to the Public for Religious
        Liberty*; Society of Jesus suppressed by Pope Clement XIV

1784   Appearance of Ethan Allen's *Reason the Only Oracle of Man*

1786   Virginia legislature passes Thomas Jefferson's "Bill for
        Establishing Religious Freedom"

1791   First Amendment to the Constitution of the United States
        guarantees that "Congress shall make no law respecting an
        establishment of religion, or prohibiting the free exercise
        thereof"

1792   James O'Kelly leads his followers into schism: the Republican
        Methodist church

1794   Western Europe receives the first volume of Thomas Paine's
        Age of Reason

1796   Holy Trinity Church (Roman Catholic) in Philadelphia
        declared schismatic

1802   Elihu Palmer's major work, *Principles of Nature*, released
        to the public

1805   Disturbing sentiments of universal salvation expressed in
        Hosea Ballou's *Treatise on Atonement*

1809   The basis for a new American church, the Disciples of Christ,
        set forth in a "Declaration and Address"

1810   Formation in Kentucky of the schismatic Cumberland
        Presbyterian church

1817   American Colonization Society organized to promote one
        possible solution to the nation's black "dilemma"

1818   Congregationalism disestablished in Connecticut

1822   The "True Dutch Reformed Church" separates from the older immigrants from Holland

1825   Liberal dissent in New England organizes itself into the American Unitarian Association

1827   At the Philadelphia Yearly Meeting, the Hicksite separation within American Quakerism begins

1830   John Winebrenner launches the General Eldership of the Church of God

1833   The last ties between church and state broken in Massachusetts; in New Mexico ecclesiastical authorities order Penitentes to conform

1834   Nativists burn Ursuline convent in Charlestown, Massachusetts

1836   Transcendental Club begins meeting in and around Boston; Orestes Brownson's *New Views* appears

1837   The Reverend Elijah P. Lovejoy, abolitionist and editor, murdered

1839   Excluded from Missouri, Mormons gather in Illinois

1840   Margaret Fuller and others bring out first issue of *The Dial*

1842   Theodore Parker writes *Discourse of Matters Pertaining to Religion*

1844   Over the issue of slavery, predominately white Methodism divides into northern and southern halves; Joseph Smith assassinated in Carthage, Illinois

1845   Baptists in the southern states withdraw from the national body

1849   Indian affairs transferred from the Department of War to the Department of Interior

1857   United States Army moves against Mormons in Utah

1860   Publication of Margaret Fuller's *Life Within and Life Without*

1861   Forty-seven southern presbyteries form the General Assembly of the Confederate States of America

1869   In Kentucky, Berea College opens as a biracial school

1873   Founding of the *Truth Seeker*, "oldest freethought paper in the world"; Felix Adler breaks with Reform Judaism; George D. Cummins breaks with the Protestant Episcopal church

1874   John William Draper publishes his popular *History of the Conflict between Religion and Science*

1875   First edition of Mary Baker Eddy's *Science and Health*

1881   Mass exodus of Jews from eastern Europe and Russia begins;
        Mary Baker Eddy establishes the Massachusetts Metaphysical
        College

1882   Anti-Oriental sentiment officially sanctioned in the Chinese
        Exclusion Act

1885   Reform rabbis adopt the "Pittsburg Platform"

1888   Beginning of Paul Carus's affiliation with the new journal,
        Open Court

1890   In *Davis* v. *Beason*, U. S. Supreme Court declares polygamy
        offensive to "the common sense of mankind"

1891   Ghost Dance religion envisions this year as great consummation
        of Indian destiny

1893   World Parliament of Religion introduces the East to the
        general public of the West

1895   Disillusioned, disaffected blacks organize the National
        Baptist Convention; P. F. Bresee launches the Church of the
        Nazarene

1898   Young Men's Buddhist Association introduced into continental
        United States (San Francisco); Francis Hodur and followers
        excommunicated by Roman Catholic Church; Union of
        Orthodox Jewish Congregations formed in opposition to liberal
        rabbinical fellowships

1899   Excommunication of nonconforming Penitentes in northern
        New Mexico

1906   Stephen S. Wise establishes his own Free Synagogue in
        New York City; Soyen Shaku's *Sermons of a Buddhist Abbott*
        published in Chicago

1914   End of the "present evil world" foreseen in the eschatology
        of early Jehovah's Witnesses or Russellites

1915   Ku Klux Klan revived; Black Baptists divide in publishing
        house dispute

1917   Mennonite General Conference issues forceful statement on
        pacifism

1918   First charter granted to the Native American Church

1920   Henry Ford begins anti-Semitic campaign in his *Dearborn
        Independent*; first edition of John Dewey's *Reconstruction
        in Philosophy*

1921   First immigration restriction law based on national origin
        percentages

1924   U. S. citizenship granted to the American Indian

1925   American Association for the Advancement of Atheism receives
        charter; right of private or denominational schooling affirmed
        in *Pierce* v. *Society of Sisters*

1929   Publication of Walter Lippmann's *Preface to Morals* and
        Joseph Wood Krutch's *Modern Temper*

1930   First edition of H. L. Mencken's iconoclastic *Treatise on
        the Gods*

1931   Followers of Charles Taze Russell officially adopt the
        designation of "Jehovah's Witnesses"

1932   Reinhold Niebuhr publishes his *Moral Man and Immoral Society*

1933   Elijah Muhammad assumes leadership of the Black Muslims;
        persecution and emigration of German Jews begins; first
        issue of *Catholic Worker* appears on May Day

1938   Father Charles E. Coughlin disseminates the *Protocols of
        the Learned Elders of Zion*

1940   In *Cantwell* v. *Connecticut* Jehovah's Witnesses win the right
        to propagandize and proselytize

1942   Thousands of Japanese Americans "relocated" in camps in
        interior America; incorporation of Buddhist Churches of
        America; Clarence Jordan starts interracial community near
        Americus, Georgia

1943   Reversing an earlier decision, the U. S. Supreme Court
        rules in favor of religious scruple against compulsory flag
        salute in the public school; Roman Catholic authorities face
        special needs of Mexican-American community

1946   Publication of Yogananda's *Autobiography of a Yogi*

1947   Billy James Hargis's Christian Crusade organized in Tulsa,
        Oklahoma

1955   Formation in Detroit of the anti-merger National Association
        of Congregational Christian Churches

1961   Walter Kaufmann's *The Faith of a Heretic* appears

1962   Himalayan Academy started in Nevada City, California

1963   Prayer and Bible-reading in the public schools declared
        unconstitutional

1965   Assassination of Malcolm X in New York City

1967   Protestant, Jewish, and Catholic scholars write *Vietnam: Crisis of Conscience*

1968   Madalyn Murray O'Hair begins radio broadcasts on the "Atheist Point of View"; assassination of Martin Luther King

1969   Mexican-American priests form PADRES organization; Tibetan monks open Meditation Center in San Francisco

1970   Arrest of Father Daniel Berrigan, S.J., Block Island, Rhode Island; Patricio F. Flores becomes first Mexican-American bishop in the Roman Catholic Church in the United States

1972   Amish school children relieved of obligation to attend public school beyond the eighth grade; "Explo 72" assembles in Cotton Bowl in Dallas, Texas

Suggested Reading

General Works

With respect to American religion generally, the readily available bibliographical apparatus makes an extensive listing here unnecessary. One's attention is directed foremost to Nelson R. Burr's two-volume *Critical Bibliography of Religion in America* (Princeton, 1961) as well as to his abridged but updated *Religion in American Life* (New York, 1971), a paperbound entry in the Goldentree Bibliographies in American History series. Dr. Burr's expansive efforts include not only the major currents of American religious history, but much of the backwater or small eddy with which the present work is directly concerned. A recent and exhaustive text by Sydney E. Ahlstrom, *A Religious History of the American People* (New Haven, 1972), contains an up-to-date and detailed bibliography; the comprehensiveness of the text itself makes the listing of other general surveys superfluous.

1	*Prologue*	*A Delineation of*
		Dissent

While America's religious history is filled with dissent, the historiography of American religion is virtually devoid of major treatments of the subject. Even a small volume such as Erik Routley's *English Religious Dissent* (Cambridge, 1960) has no genuine analogue on the American side. This absence may be partially accounted for by Routley's comment that since the United States has no established church, the arena of dissent is transferred to politics and morals. He adds, "A history of American Dissent would be a psychological and political story rather than a religious one" (p. 82). Obviously I have rejected this position, even while conceding that the problem of defining religious dissent in America is fraught with difficulty — for the very reasons that Routley suggests.

In 1934 John M. Mecklin published *The Story of American Dissent* (reprinted Port Washington, N. Y., 1970) that dealt exclusively with religious dissent. Largely limited to the activities of the Baptists, Methodists, and Presbyterians, his account fails to do justice to the full diversity, even perversity, of religious dissent in American history. A generation after Mecklin, book titles speaking of "American dissent" would be understood as referring to the moral and political arenas noted by Routley. For example, *Dissent: Explorations in the History of American Radicalism* (DeKalb, Illinois, 1968), edited by Alfred F. Young, is heavily political, though it contains a brief but important article by Herbert G. Gutman on "Protestantism and the American Labor Movement" and a deeply felt account of "Black Radicalism: The Road from Montgomery" by Vincent Harding. Religion as the avenue of dissent is even more subdued in Kenneth Keniston's *Youth and Dissent: The Rise of a New Opposition* (New York, 1971). The history and vitality of religious dissent may be best preserved in the periodical literature; fortunately, the often obscure or rare journals of earlier years are being reprinted: for example, the two series issued by Greenwood Publishing Company, and the collection called "Protest, Controversy and Dissent" issued by University Microfilms. Many of the journals in these collections emerge from religious orientations that cannot be categorized simply as "left" or "right," as "perfectionist" or "anarchist," but can be uniformly classified as sustained examples of dissent. One should also note the volumes reissued by the Kraus Reprint Company under the title, "American Religious Radicalism in the Nineteenth Century."

The quotations from Nietzsche's *Genealogy of Morals* (New York, 1912 edition) are from the preface to that volume. Kierkegaard's *Attack Upon "Christendom"* (Boston, 1956) is cited, p. 108 et passim.

2   *The Schismatics*   *Sinners Against*
                               Love

On the deep cultural fracture between the secular and the sacred see Martin E. Marty, *The Modern Schism: Three Paths to the Secular* (London, 1960). On the complex subject of organizational life and ecclesiastical separations in America, everyone needs help. Quick orientation is given historically in Frank S. Mead, *Handbook of Denominations in the United*

States (Nashville, latest revision, 1970); theologically in F. E. Mayer, *The Religious Bodies of America* (Saint Louis, 1954); and structurally in the annual *Yearbook of American Churches*, currently edited by Constant H. Jacquet, Jr. (New York).

Piety. On the outburst of piety related to the Great Awakening, the literature has grown rapidly in recent years. See, for example, Alan Heimert and Perry Miller, *The Great Awakening: Documents Illustrating the Crisis and Its Consequences* (Indianapolis, 1967); David S. Lovejoy, *Religious Enthusiasm and the Great Awakening* (Englewood Cliffs, N. J., 1969); Richard L. Bushman, *The Great Awakening: Documents on the Revival of Religion, 1740–1745* (New York, 1970); and, Edwin S. Gaustad, *The Great Awakening in New England* (Chicago, reprinted, 1968). On Isaac Backus see William G. McLoughlin, *Isaac Backus and the American Pietistic Tradition* (Boston, 1967) as well as the same author's monumental study of *New England Dissent, 1630–1833* (2 vols.; Cambridge, Mass., 1971). On the schismatic effects of this pietistic strain, one should consult C. C. Goen's *Revivalism and Separatism in New England, 1740–1800* (New Haven, 1962). The quotations from Backus are taken from his own *History of New England* . . . (2 vols.; Newton, Mass., 1871) 2:23lf.; from Alvah Hovey, *A Memoir of the Life and Times of the Rev. Isaac Backus, A. M.* (Boston, 1859), p. 334f. and p. 220f.; and from the McLoughlin biography noted above, p. 42.

Liberty. The development of religious liberty in the United States has such significance that it has provoked many detailed studies of that process, colony by colony or decade by decade. Two general works only will be noted here: the older work by Sanford H. Cobb, *The Rise of Religious Liberty in America: A History* (New York, 1902); and the painstaking three-volume study of Anson Phelps Stokes, *Church and State in the United States* (New York, 1950), condensed into a single volume and revised by Leo Pfeffer (New York, 1964). The basic study of James O'Kelly is W. E. MacClenny's *Life of Rev. James O'Kelly* . . . (Raleigh, N. C., 1910); O'Kelly's words are quoted from pp. 66, 94, and 249f. The best history of Methodism in this country is the three-volume *History of American Methodism* edited by Emory S. Bucke (New York, 1964); quotations have been taken from Frederick A. Norwood's "The Church Takes Shape," pp. 429, 436, 445, and 448. Jesse Lee's *Short History of the Methodists in the United States of America* (Baltimore, 1810) treats the O'Kelly schism, pp. 176–80.

Frontier. Peter G. Mode's *Frontier Spirit in American Christianity* (New York, 1923) remains the basic treatment of this motif in domestic religion, though one should also consult Walter B. Posey's *Frontier Mission: a History of Religion West of the Southern Appalachians to 1861* (Lexington, 1966). Posey's *Presbyterian Church in the Old Southwest 1778–1838* (Richmond, 1952) provides useful background, especially in chaps. 3 and 4. Even more extensive background is available in E. T. Thompson, *Presbyterians in the South* 1 (Richmond, 1963), and important documents are contained in W. W. Sweet, *Religion on the American Frontier: The Presbyterians* (New York, reprinted 1964). B. W. McDonnold's older *History of the Cumberland Presbyterian Church* (Nashville, 1888), p. 74 of which has been cited, is now superseded by Ben M. Barrus et al., *A People Called Cumberland Presbyterians* (Memphis, 1972). The principal source utilized in this account is F. R. Cossitt, *The Life and Times of Rev. Finis Ewing . . .* (Louisville, 3d ed., 1853), pp. 199, 296, and 484–85; the long quotation is taken from the appendix, pp. 480–82.

Evangelicalism. For a general view of the evangelical spirit in nineteenth-century American religion, it would be difficult to improve on Baird himself; see his *Religion in the United States of America* (New York, reprinted 1969), also available in an abridged edition with introduction by Henry Warner Bowden, *Religion in America* (New York, 1970). One may likewise consult Baird's *Christian Retrospect and Register* (New York, 1851). The latest general account of the Episcopal communion in America is Raymond W. Albright's *A History of the Protestant Episcopal Church* (New York, 1964). For the tensions between the Evangelical party and its opposite in that church, see G. R. Balleine, *A History of the Evangelical Party in the Church of England* (London, 1951), and George E. De Mille, *The Catholic Movement in the American Episcopal Church* (Philadelphia, revised 1950). Quotations in this section are taken from A. M. Cummins, *Memoir of George David Cummins, D. D., First Bishop of the Reformed Episcopal Church* (New York, 1878), pp. 288, 294, 297–98, 323, 329, 360, 364, 413, and 419–20. Excerpts have also been taken from Benjamin Aycrigg, ed., *Memoirs of the Reformed Episcopal Church and of the Protestant Episcopal Church . . .* (New York, 1880), pp. 141 and 154; see all of chap. 12 therein on "Schism and Separation."

Ethnicity. For an appreciation of the ethnic strength in American history, one should become familiar with portions of the vast literature on immigration; a convenient point of departure is Maldwyn A. Jones, *American Immigration* (Chicago, 1960). Michael Novak's recent *The Rise of the Unmeltable Ethnics* (New York, 1972) suggests that ethnic strength is a part of America's present no less than of its past. Histories of

Roman Catholicism in America abound, but one may rely most confidently upon the many works of John Tracy Ellis. Several aspects of the ethnic concern within this ecclesiastical tradition are explored in *Roman Catholicism and the American Way of Life*, edited by Thomas T. McAvoy (Notre Dame, 1960). Accounts of the Polish schism include Paul Fox, *The Polish National Catholic Church* (Scranton, 1961), and Robert W. Janowski, *The Growth of a Church: a Historical Documentary* (Scranton, 1965). Quotations are taken from Theodore Andrews, *The Polish National Catholic Church in America and Poland* (London, 1953), pp. 26, 29. See also the *New Catholic Encyclopedia* (Washington, 1967) 11:505–6. The liturgical literature and some historical material of this church are available from its Book Department Mission Fund, 1006 Pittston Avenue, Scranton, Pennsylvania, 18505.

Race. For useful background see Oscar Handlin's *Race and Nationality in American Life* (New York, 1957); Thomas F. Gossett, *Race: The History of an Idea in America* (Dallas, 1963); and Winthrop D. Jordan, *White over Black: American Attitudes Toward the Negro 1550–1812* (Chapel Hill, 1968). Reprint houses have made available vast quantities of history and literature pertaining to the American Negro; see, for example, the several series issued by Arno Press and the *New York Times*. Regarding the Negro and his religion in America see E. Franklin Frazier, *The Negro Church in America* (New York, reprinted 1970); Hart M. Nelson et al., *The Black Church in America* (New York, 1971); and Carter G. Woodson's still useful *History of the Negro Church* (Washington, revised 1945), p. 236 of which has been used in the text. White-black relationships in a religious context are treated in H. Shelton Smith, *In his Image, But . . . : Racism in Southern Religion, 1780–1910* (Durham, 1972); in Joseph C. Hough, Jr., *Black Power and White Protestants* (New York, 1968); and, in D. E. Harrell, Jr., *White Sects and Black Men in the Recent South* (Nashville, 1971). Quotations in the text are from Lewis G. Jordan, *Negro Baptist History U. S. A.* (Nashville, 1930), pp. 122, 124, 132–33, and 137; from Benjamin G. Brawley, *Negro Builders and Heroes* (Chapel Hill, reprinted 1965), pp. 201–2; and, from E. C. Morris, *Sermons, Addresses and Reminiscences and Important Correspondence . . .* (Nashville, 1901), p. 71. For additional data on black Baptists see E. A. Freeman, *Epoch of Negro Baptists and the Foreign Mission Board* (Kansas City, 1953), and O. D. Pelt and R. L. Smith, *The Story of the National Baptists* (New York, 1960).

Ecumenism. The basic treatments of the ecumenical movement are Ruth Rouse and S. C. Neill, *A History of the Ecumenical Movement*

1517–1948 (Philadelphia, revised 1967), and Harold E. Fey, ed., *The Ecumenical Advance: A History of the Ecumenical Movement 1948–1968* (Philadelphia, 1970). On the general history of Congregationalism, see Gaius G. Atkins and Frederick L. Fagley, *History of American Congregationalism* (Boston, 1942), and more recently, Douglas Horton, *The United Church of Christ: Its Origins, Organizations, and Role in the World Today* (New York, 1962). Two doctoral dissertations have examined with great care the struggle and schism concerning Congregationalism's latest merger: Alan B. Peabody, "A Study of the Controversy in Congregationalism over Merger with the Evangelical and Reformed Church" (Syracuse University, 1964), and Charles E. Harvey, "Individualism and Ecumenical Thought: The Merger Controversy in Congregationalism, 1937–1961" (University of California, Riverside, 1968). Quotations are taken from Peabody, pp. 53lff., 540, 630–31, and 635; quotations from Douglas Horton's "Of Equability and Perseverance in Well Doing" are from Harvey, pp. 267–68. Malcolm K. Burton's *Destiny for Congregationalism* (Oklahoma City, 1953) has been utilized, pp. 199–202, 224.

3   *The Heretics*   *Sinners Against Faith*

Martin E. Marty's *The Infidel: Free Thought and American Religion* (Cleveland, 1961), p. 175, is cited in the first paragraph. For the quotations from Chesterton, see his *Heretics* (London, 1905), pp. 4–5, 7, and 288–89; see also his *Orthodoxy* (London, 1908). These volumes have no precise parallel on the American scene, though there have been several efforts of late to define the prevailing consensus or the civil religion in America. Note particularly these works: Elwyn A. Smith, ed., *The Religion of the Republic* (Philadelphia, 1971); Conrad Cherry, ed., *God's New Israel: Religious Interpretations of American Destiny* (Englewood Cliffs, 1971); Winthrop S. Hudson, ed., *Nationalism and Religion in America: Concepts of American Identity and Mission* (New York, 1970); and Robert T. Handy, *A Christian American: Protestant Hopes and Historical Realities* (New York, 1971). For the full sweep of religious thinking in the United States see William A. Clebsch, *American Religious Thought: A History* (Chicago, 1973). For a helpful theological framework see Sydney E. Ahlstrom, comp., *Theology in America: The Major Protestant Voices from Puritanism to Neo-Orthodoxy* (Indianapolis, 1967); Daniel D. Williams, *What Present-Day Theologians are Thinking* (New York, revised 1967); and, Herbert W. Richardson, *Toward an*

American Theology (New York, 1967). On those "tender souls trapped in parochial sectarian strife" see G. H. Shriver, ed., *American Religious Heretics: Formal and Informal Trials* (Nashville, 1966).

A Reasonable World: The attraction of a religion of reason is explicated in such standard works as Herbert M. Morais, *Deism in Eighteenth Century America* (New York, 1934); Stow Persons, *Free Religion, an American Faith* (New Haven, 1947); Conrad Wright, *The Beginnings of Unitarianism in America* (Boston, 1955); and Adrienne Koch and Frank Freidel, eds., *American Enlightenment* (New York, 1965). Benjamin Franklin's youthful dissertation, of which only two copies survived, is found in L. W. Labaree, ed., *The Papers of Benjamin Franklin* (New Haven, 1959) 1:58–71; the quotations are from pp. 57, 61. Ethan Allen's *Reason the Only Oracle of Man*, originally published in Bennington, Vermont, by Haswell & Russell, has been reproduced in facsimile, with an introduction by John Pell, by Scholars' Facsimiles & Reprints, New York, 1940; pp. 83–84, 200, and 474–75 of this edition are quoted. The second edition of Elihu Palmer's *Principles of Nature; Or, A Development of the Moral Causes of Happiness and Misery Among the Human Species* (New York, 1802) has been excerpted from these pages: iii, 31–32, 37, 143, 270–71, 321, and 324. Paine's *Age of Reason* is included in Maurice D. Conway, ed., *The Writings of Thomas Paine* (New York, reprinted 1967); quotations are from vol. 4, pp. 23, 33–34, 45, 151.

A Romantic World. So literate were the romanticists and the Transcendentalists that the bibliographical possibilities are overwhelming. Standard editions that exist for many of the New England coterie may be consulted with ease. For romanticism within the bounds of orthodoxy, the treatments are fewer; see Ronald V. Wells, *Three Christian Transcendentalists* (New York, 1943), and James H. Nichols, *Romanticism in American Theology: Nevin and Schaff at Mercersburg* (Chicago, 1961). The words of Andrews Norton and Francis Bowen are found in Perry Miller's authoritative anthology, *The Transcendentalists* (Cambridge, 1950), pp. 210–13, 177; Miller's own words are from p. 9. Brownson's corpus has been prepared by H. F. Brownson in a twenty-volume edition, *The Works of Orestes A. Brownson* (Detroit, 1882–1888). Brownson's autobiography, *The Convert*, appearing in vol. 5, is quoted from pp. 75–76. *New Views*, in vol. 6, has quotations from pp. 5, 52, and 55; see also vol. 5, pp. 64, 77–78. The biography by Arthur M. Schlesinger, Jr., *Orestes A. Brownson: A Pilgrim's Progress* (Boston, 1939) is valuable, especially pp. 44–50. For the life of transcendentalism's leading feminist see Mason Wade, *Margaret Fuller: Whet-*

stone of Genius (New York, 1940), and Arthur W. Brown, *Margaret Fuller* (New York, 1964). The reminiscences of her three friends are from *Memoirs of Margaret Fuller Ossoli* (2 vols; Boston, 1852) 1:132–36, 308f.; 2:12–14. Fuller's own meditation is from her *Life Without and Life Within . . .* (Boston, 1860; reprinted 1970), p. 277. The early issues of *The Dial* are in print once more (New York, 1961). The most extensive biography of Theodore Parker is John Weiss, *Life and Correspondence of Theodore Parker* (2 vols.; New York, reprinted 1969); see 1:184, 452. Clarke's comment on Parker is from his discourse delivered in 1860, *A Look at the Life of Theodore Parker* (Boston, 1910), pp. 17–18. Items from Parker's 1841 sermon on the "Transient and permanent in Christianity" are found in the Perry Miller anthology noted above, pp. 270, 272, 276, 277, 281. The final quotation of Parker's is from his *Discourse of Matters Pertaining to Religion* (Boston, 1842), p. 483. Frothingham's 1876 history, *Transcendentalism in New England*, was reprinted by the University of Pennsylvania Press in 1959 and again in 1972. In this entire area, one may also profitably consult William R. Hutchison's *The Transcendentalist Ministers* (New Haven, 1959).

A Scientific World. In addition to the Draper opus noted below, one should be familiar with the standard treatment by Andrew D. White, *A History of the Warfare of Science with Theology in Christendom* (New York, 1896), and with the more recent account by Edward A. White, *Science and Religion in American Thought* (Stanford, 1952). The best biography of Draper is Donald Fleming, *John William Draper and the Religion of Science* (Philadelphia, 1950). Draper's own *History of the Conflict between Religion and Science* has been many times reprinted; for the specific page references (v, vii, x–xii, 52, 62, 365–67, and 328) see the 1889 edition in the International Scientific Series (New York). On the life of Powell see W. C. Darrah, *Powell of the Colorado* (Princeton, 1951), and Wallace Stegner, *Beyond the Hundredth Meridian: John Wesley Powell and the Second Opening of the West* (Boston, 1954). Powell's words are taken from Darrah's volume, pp. 356, 360, 379–80. See also Powell's article on "The Evolution of Religion," in *The Monist* 8 (1898):203, 204; and Powell's *Truth and Error, Or, The Science of Intellection* (Chicago, 1898), pp. 4–5, 382–90. Paul Carus was a prolific writer. The most relevant works for his elevation of science into a religion are his *Dawn of a New Religious Era* (Chicago, 1916), pp. 25, 26, 46f.; his *God: An Enquiry into the Nature of Man's highest Ideal and a Solution of the Problem from the Standpoint of Science* (Chicago, 1908), p. 82ff.; and his *Religion of Science* (Chicago, 1896). This entire cultural phenomenon is ably described in Paul A. Carter, *The Spiritual Crisis of the Gilded Age* (DeKalb, 1971).

An Egocentric World. When science is not elevated to the status of religion, attempts may then be made to establish religion upon firm, practicable, scientific foundations. Some of that effort is evident in the several strains described in Charles S. Braden, *Spirits in Rebellion: The Rise and Development of New Thought* (Dallas, 1963); in J. Stillson Judah, *The History and Philosophy of the Metaphysical Movements in America* Philadelphia, 1967); and especially in Donald Meyer, *The Positive Thinkers* (New York, 1965); the quotation from Meyer is found on p. 293. Mrs Eddy's description of Christian Science is from her *Miscellaneous Writings 1883–1896* (Boston, 1897), p. 336. Quotations from the first edition of *Science and Health* (Boston, 1875) may be found on pp. 387, 391, and 394. Quotations from the "Key to the Scriptures" are from modern editions of *Science and Health*, pp. 579, 584, and the concluding section, "Fruitage." Mark Twain's criticism is in his *Christian Science . . .* (New York, 1907), p. 75. Robert Peel's *Christian Science: Its Encounter with American Culture* (New York, 1965) treats the movement in its cultural context. For Psychiana, one is dependent chiefly on the movement's own writings, though chapters on the sect can be found in Marcus Bach, *These Have Found a Faith* (Indianapolis, 1946), and Charles S. Braden, *They Also Believe* (New York, 1949). Pages 98 and 218 of Robinson's *Life Story of Frank B. Robinson* (Moscow, Idaho, 1934) have been excerpted, and a booklet from the Psychiana headquarters called *Here is Your Word Study of Psychiana* (1941, revised 1949) has also been utilized, pp. 2, 4, and 10.

A Humanistic World. Humanism is seen at its most eloquent in George Santayana's *Life of Reason* (New York, 1905–6), especially in the third volume of that series, *Reason in Religion*. Persuasive exposition is also found in Charles F. Potter's *Humanism, a New Religion* (New York, 1930) and his *Humanizing Religion* (New York, 1933), while sharp criticism from a theistic stance can be found in L. J. A. Mercier, *The Challenge of Humanism* (New York, 1933), and in Arthur H. Dakin, *Man the Measure: an Essay on Humanism as Religion* (Princeton, 1939). Lippmann's *Preface to Morals* (New York, 1929) has citations from pp. 137, 150, and 153–64. See pp. 114 and 132 of his *Public Philosophy* (Boston, 1955) for the source of comments taken from that volume. Citations to Krutch's *Modern Temper* (New York, 1929) are from pp. 31, 33, 35–36, and 159, while those to his *Human Nature and the Human Condition* (New York, 1959) are from pp. 78–95, 98–99, 167, 187, and 200. Quotations from Dewey's *On Experience, Nature, and*

Freedom are from the edition prepared by R. J. Bernstein (New York, 1960), pp. 66–67. See the enlarged edition of Dewey's *Reconstruction in Philosophy* (Boston, 1957), pp. 124 and 174ff.; quotations from his *A Common Faith* (New Haven, 1934) may be found on pp. 42, 44, 56–57. Bertrand Russell's observation is from his familiar *History of Western Philosophy* (New York, 1945), p. 828.

A Skeptical World. The popular purveyors of skepticism have their analogue in works designed for a more limited audience; for example, see Paul Elmer More, *The Sceptical Approach to Religion* (Princeton, 1934), and George Santayana, *Scepticism and Animal Faith* (New York, 1955). Neither of these had anything like the swift popularity of Mencken's *Treatise on the Gods* (New York, 1930), which went through ten printings before it was revised in 1945; the revision has likewise had repeated reprintings. All Mencken quotations are from the revised edition, pp. vi, 192–93, 176, 230–31, 243–45, 247, 257, 265, 292. Walter Kaufmann's *Faith of a Heretic* (New York, 1961) is quoted, pp. 60, 104, and 130; the dialogue with Satan is from his *Critique of Religion and Philosophy* (New York, 1958), pp. 243–55, while his comment on the philosopher's vocation is from "The Faith of a Heretic," *Harper's Magazine* 218, no. 1305 (February, 1959):39. Atheism is, of course, not the precise equivalent of skepticism, but most of America's atheists appear to concentrate on what they do not believe, moving themselves thereby closer to a skeptical position. Madalyn Murray O'Hair is preceded in her particular heretical tradition by Woolsey Teller, *The Atheism of Astronomy* (New York, 1938); Joseph Lewis, *An Atheist Manifesto* (New York, 1954); and others. Undated leaflets published by the Truth Seeker Company of New York constitute the source of the miscellaneous titles on atheism. Mrs. O'Hair's own writings emanate from the American Atheist Press, Box 2117, Austin, Texas. See especially her *What on Earth is an Atheist?* (1969), pp. 13–14, 38, and 52. And see the collection that she edited for Arno Press (New York, 1971), particularly the several atheist magazines for the period 1927–70, now available in a single volume. The Douglas quotation is from *Zorach* v. *Clauson*, 343 US 306 (1952).

4   *The Misfits*   *Sinners Against Society*

The relationships between religion and culture — the tensions, conflicts, and mutual dependencies — have received ample attention from anthropologists, sociologists, political scientists, historians, philosophers, theologians, and busy churchmen. One approach to these several avenues is through the special issues of *The Annals* of the American Academy of Political and Social Science devoted to religion in American society: vol. 256 (March, 1948), vol. 332 (November, 1960), and vol. 387 (January, 1970). See also the essays collected in John Cogley, ed., *Religion in America* (New York, 1958); Harold Stahmer, ed., *Religion & Contemporary Society* (New York, 1963); Robert E. Lee and Martin E. Marty, eds., *Religion and Social Conflict* (New York, 1964); and Philip E. Hammond and Benton Johnson, eds., *American Mosaic: Social Patterns of Religion in the United States* (New York, 1970).

The Destroyed. Reliable introductions to the American Indians include William T. Hagan, *American Indians* (Chicago, 1961), and John Collier, *The Indians of North America* (New York, 1947); Collier's statement is from p. 224 of his book. The Kansas paper advocating extermination, the *Junction City Weekly Union* for 19 June 1869, is cited in R. W. Mardock, *The Reformers and the American Indian* (Columbia, Mo., 1971), p. 88. The classic account of the Ghost Dance is James Mooney's *The Ghost-Dance Religion and the Sioux Outbreak of 1890*, originally issued in 1896 by the Government Printing Office, now republished (1965) by the University of Chicago Press. David H. Miller's *Ghost Dance* (New York, 1959) is a more recent account, with excellent bibliography. The goals of Nebraska's Native American Church are given in Hazel W. Hertzberg, *The Search for an American Indian Identity* (Syracuse, 1971), p. 277. On the peyote cult in general see Vittorio Lanternari, *The Religion of the Oppressed* (London, 1963); J. L. Slotkin, *The Peyote Religion: A Study in Indian-White Relations* (Glencoe, 1956); Weston La Barre, *The Peyote Cult* (New York, revised 1969); and two popular "inside" treatments by Carlos Castaneda, *The Teachings of Don Juan* (Berkeley, 1968) and *A Separate Reality* (New York, 1971). Indian resistance to the religious use of peyote is evident in the life of the Sioux, Charles Alexander Eastman; see his small volume, *The Soul of the Indian* (New York, reprinted 1971). Weston La Barre's *The Ghost Dance* (New York, 1970), while it does briefly treat that specific Indian ritual, is mainly concerned to examine all religion from a harshly critical anthropological and psychological point of view — with the hope that modern man might surrender all forms of "antic self-cozening ghost dance."

The Exiled. On Roger Williams see the excellent introduction with helpful editing of Williams' crabbed prose by Perry Miller, *Roger Williams: His Contribution to the American Tradition* (New York, 1962); the most authoritative interpretation of Williams thought in that area that resulted in his exile is Edmund S. Morgan's *Roger Williams: The Church and the State* (New York, 1967). For the general history of Judaism in America as well as something of what it means to be a practicing Jew in this country see Nathan Glazer, *American Judaism* (Chicago, revised 1972); Jacob Neusner, *American Judaism: Adventure in Modernity* (New York, 1972); and, Joseph L. Blau, *Judaism in America* (Chicago, forthcoming). On the unlovelier anti-Semitic side see the classic treatment by John Higham, *Strangers in the Land: Patterns of American Nativism 1860–1925* (New Brunswick, 1955), as well as these newer studies: Arthur Gilbert, *A Jew in Christian America* (New York, 1966); Charles J. Tull, *Father Coughlin and the New Deal* (Syracuse, 1965); and Judd L. Teller, *Strangers and Natives: The Evolution of the American Jew from 1921 to the Present* (New York, 1968). Coughlin's comments on Pius XI and Pius XII are voiced in an interview found in *American Heritage* (October 1972), pp. 40, 105. For Stephen Wise see his autobiography, *Challenging Years* (New York, 1949), and Albert Vorspan, *Giants of Justice* (New York, 1960). The source of the quotation from Wise is Alex J. Goldman, *Giants of Faith: Great American Rabbis* (New York, 1964), p. 188. The basic source for Mormon history is B. H. Roberts, *History of the Church of Jesus Christ of Latter-day Saints* (7 vols.; Salt Lake City, reprinted 1964); see particularly 1: 372–76 and 7:478. One should also consult the new periodical *Dialogue: A Journal of Mormon Thought*, itself a worthy example of responsible dissent. In vol. 5, no. 1 (Spring 1970), Richard Bushman comments that Mormons, Indians, Catholics, and Masons operated in nineteenth-century American literature as a foil, "the picture of what a good American was not" (p. 58). In this regard also see David Brion Davis, *Fear of Conspiracy: Images of Un-American Subversion from the Revolution to the Present* (Ithaca, 1971); and the readings edited by R. O. Curry and T. M. Brown, *Conspiracy: The Fear of Subversion in American History* (New York, 1972).

The Feared. See pp. 348–49 of Edward McNall Burns's *American Idea of Mission* (New Brunswick, 1957) for his delineation of the American self-image. On black nationalism, one should consult E. U. Essien-Udom, *Black Nationalism: A Search for an Identity in America* (Chicago, 1962), and Louis E. Lomax, *When the Word is Given . . .* (Cleveland, 1963). The words of Alexander Crummel are found in John H. Bracey, Jr., et al., *Black Nationalism in America* (Indianapolis, 1970), pp. 133–34, 138–39. That same volume, p. 173, is the source of the excerpt from Bishop Henry M. Turner's sermon, "The Negro has not Sense Enough." See C. Eric Lincoln, *The Black Muslims* (Boston, 1961),

pp. 96–97, for the remarks of Malcolm X on separate statehood. Elijah
Muhammad's *Message to the Blackman in America* (Chicago, 1965) is
cited, pp. 220–34. The call of Malcolm X for America to repent is
in the Lomax volume noted above, p. 158. Also see the biography
by Peter Goldman, *The Death and Life of Malcolm X* (New York, 1972).
For Reinhold Niebuhr one can usefully begin with the topical essays
in Charles W. Kegley and Robert W. Bretall, *Reinhold Niebuhr: His
Religious, Social and Political Thought* (New York, 1961), cited, p. 73.
Of Niebuhr's own works during his Marxist phase see particularly his
Moral Man and Immoral Society (New York, 1932) and his *Reflections
on the End of an Era* (New York, 1934); p. 88 of the former volume
contains the remark about nations crucifying their moral rebels. For
the religious and cultural context in which Dorothy Day wrote see
Aaron I. Abell, *American Catholicism and Social Action* (Notre Dame,
1963); David J. O'Brien, *American Catholics and Social Reform* (New
York, 1968); and Philip Gleason, *Catholicism in America* (New York,
1970). Dorothy Day's *From Union Square to Rome* was published in
1938 and her autobiography, *The Long Loneliness*, in 1960. But the
major source is the *Catholic Worker* itself, now happily reprinted
(Westport, Conn., 1970) with a delightful introduction by Dwight
MacDonald. Quotations have been taken from that introduction, from
the new preface by Dorothy Day, and from vol. 1, no. 8 (1 February
1934):4. Also see the recent history, *A Harsh and Dreadful Love: Dorothy
Day and the Catholic Worker Movement* by William D. Miller (New
York, 1972). Robert McAfee Brown's reflections on Daniel Berrigan's
capture are in the *Christian Century* 89, no. 20 (17 May 1972):572–75.
Several volumes have recently appeared on the Berrigan dissent. See
especially these three: Jack Nelson and Ronald J. Ostrow, *The FBI
and the Berrigans* (New York, 1972); Stephen Halpert and Tom Murray,
eds., *Witness of the Berrigans* (Garden City, N. Y., 1972); and William
O'Rourke, *The Harrisburg 7 and the New Catholic Left* (New York,
1972). Daniel Berrigan's latest books are also most relevant: *Absurd
Convictions, Modest Hopes* (New York, 1972); and *America is Hard to
Find* (Garden City, N. Y., 1972).

   The Ridiculed. The pessimistic millennialist stand against the confident consensus is described in the E. A. Smith, W. S. Hudson, and
R. T. Handy volumes noted in the first paragraph above under chap.
3. Also see Paul C. Nagel, *This Sacred Trust: American Nationality
1798–1898* (New York, 1971). Excellent background on millennialism
is provided in C. Norman Kraus, *Dispensationalism in America: Its Rise
and Development* (Richmond, 1958); Sylvia Trupp, ed., *The Millennial*

Dreams in Action (The Hague, 1962); and especially, Ernest Lee Tuveson, *Redeemer Nation: The Idea of America's Millennial Role* (Chicago, 1968). All quotations from William Miller are from his *Evidence from Scripture and History of the Second Coming of Christ* . . . (Boston, 1841), Introduction and Lecture 1. "This Movement that began in a whisper . . ." is from LeRoy Edwin Froom, *Movement of Destiny* (Washington, D.C., 1971), p. 662. For the context of Adventism see Whitney R. Cross, *The Burned-Over District* (Ithaca, 1950), and for another example of a denominational journal of quiet dissent see the Adventist *Spectrum.* Russell's predictions are from his *Millennial Dawn,* vol. 1, *The Plan of the Ages* (Allegheny, Pa., 1902):72–75, 91, 345. The movement's own history, *Jehovah's Witnesses in the Divine Purpose* (New York, 1959), is cited from pp. 55 and 291. Recent millennial assertions are from *The Nations Shall Know That I Am Jehovah — How?* (New York, 1971), pp. 406–7; and the booklet, *When All Nations Collide Head-On with God* (Brooklyn, 1971), pp. 22, 23, 26, 27. On the radical right see such studies as these: Daniel Bell, *The Radical Right* (New York, 1963); Mark Sherwin, *The Extremists* (New York, 1963); Harry and Bonaro Overstreet, *The Strange Tactics of Extremism* (New York, 1964); Brooks R. Walker, *The Christian Fright Peddlers* (New York, 1964); and Erling T. Jorstad, *The Politics of Doomsday: Fundamentalists of the Far Right* (Nashville, 1970). All Hargis quotations are from John Harold Redekop, *The American Far Right: A Case Study of Billy James Hargis and Christian Crusade* (Grand Rapids, Mich., 1968); see especially pp. 20, 27, 34–37, 50, 59, and 201. Hal Lindsey's *The Late Great Planet Earth* (Grand Rapids, 1970) is the most successful current declaration of how and when Armageddon will come.

The Patronized. For early American flirtations with Eastern thought see Arthur E. Christy, *The Orient in American Transcendentalism: A Study of Emerson, Thoreau and Alcott* (New York, 1932). Abundant materials concerning the World Parliament itself are contained in the massive two volumes edited by John Henry Barrows, *The World Parliament of Religions* (Chicago, 1893); Vivekenanda's comments are from vol. 2:968. On Buddhism's entry into America see Hal Bridges, *American Mysticism* (New York, 1970), chap. 6. The sudden revival of interest in things Eastern is fully explored in Jacob Needleman, *The New Religions* (New York, 1970). For the Mexican-Americans see Julian Samora, ed., *La Raza: Forgotten Americans* (Notre Dame, 1966), particularly chap. 2 by John A. Wagner; and Leo Grebler et al., *The Mexican-American People: The Nation's Second Largest Minority* (Glencoe, 1970), especially chap. 19 by Patrick H. McNamara. For the Penitentes the following sources are instructive: Alice C. Henderson, *Brothers of Light: the Penitentes of the Southwest* (Chicago, 1962); Bill Tate, *The Penitentes of the Sangre de Cristos: An American Tragedy* (Truchas, N. M., 2d ed. 1967); Lorayne Horka-Follick, *Los Hermanos Penitentes* (New York, 1969); and Angelico Chavez, "The Penitentes of New Mexico," *New Mexico Historical Review* 29, no. 2 (April 1954):97–123. I am grateful to my colleague, Carlos E. Cortés, for calling to my attention the dissenting nature of the persisting Penitente ritual. The Salpointe quotation is from the Horka-Follick book, p. 153. The comment that the Church has "plenty to do to attend to her own business" is cited by Patrick McNamara from *The Tidings* (22 October 1937, p. 8) in Grebler, p. 458.

The Sentimentalized. The Mennonite tradition in broadest theological perspective is portrayed in George H. Williams, *Spiritual and Anabaptist Writers* (Philadelphia, 1957). That tradition in America, but with some European background, is found in John C. Wenger, *The Mennonite Church in America* (Scottdale, Pa., 1966). John A. Hostetler is the principal authority on America's Amish: see his *Amish Society* (Baltimore, revised 1968). On the pacifist issue consult Peter Brock's *Pacifism in the United States from the Colonial Era to the First World War* (Princeton, 1968) as well as the Random House reprint series, "The Peace Movement in America." Among the Mennonites specifically see J. S. Hartzler, *Mennonites in the World War, or Nonresistance Under Test* (Scottdale, Pa., 1922), citations from pp. 26–27, 38, 64–65, 150–51; and Guy F. Hershberger's *The Mennonite Church in the Second World War* (Scottdale, Pa., 1951) as well as his long article, "Conscientious Objector," in the *Mennonite Encyclopedia* 1 (Scottdale, Pa., 1955): 691–99. The most thorough study of Amish educational tribulation is that of Harrell R. Rodgers, Jr., *Community Conflict, Public Opinion and the Law: The Amish Dispute in Iowa* (Columbus, O., 1969). But see also Donald A. Erickson, "The Plain People vs. The Common Schools," *Saturday Review* (19 November 1966), pp. 85–87f. The *Wisconsin* v. *Yoder* decision is found in *U. S. Supreme Court Reports* 32, no. 1 (12 June 1972):15–44. The Amish on Broadway is briefly noted by Charles Burkhart in the *Mennonite Quarterly Review* 31, no. 2 (April 1957):140–42.

6   *Epilogue*   *New Directions in*
                                    Religious Dissent

Theodore Roszak's widely read volume, *The Making of a Counter Culture*
(Garden City, 1969), is very suggestive concerning the possible new
directions of dissent. The description of the march on the Pentagon
is from *The East Village Other*, cited in Roszak, p. 124; Roszak's own
words are from pp. 8, 63, 105, and 146. Robert McAfee Brown,
Abraham J. Heschel, and Michael Novak collaborated in 1967 to produce *Vietnam: Crisis of Conscience* (New York). Kenneth Kenniston's
Youth and Dissent, already noted in the suggested reading for chap.
1, offers a typology of youthful dissent on pp. 146ff. For the counterat-
tack of the establishment against dissent, especially political, see Jethro
K. Lieberman, *How the Government Breaks the Law* (New York, 1972).
Chaps. 4. "Journey to the East," and 5, "The Counterfeit Infinity,"
of Roszak are both useful in assessing the contemporary rejection of
rationalism and turn toward mystery. See also Hal Bridges's *American
Mysticism*, already cited, chaps. 5–8. On community see such recent
volumes as Robert S. Fogarty, *American Utopianism* (Itasca, Ill., 1972)
and Ron E. Roberts, *The New Communes: Coming Together in America*
(Englewood Cliffs, N. J., 1971). To keep up with this rapidly expand-
ing area, one should also read the bimonthly periodical, *Modern Utopian:
The Magazine of Social Change*, published by the Starr King Center,
2441 Le Conte Avenue, Berkeley, California 94709. I acknowledge
with gratitude the kindness of my colleague, Robert V. Hine, for
making available to me portions of his vast collection on modern communes. For the underground church see the chapter by Theodore M.
Steeman, pp. 713–48, in Donald R. Cutler, ed., *The Religious Situation
1969* (Boston, 1969); and Garry Wills, *Bare Ruined Choirs* (New York,
1972). In this drive toward mutual relationships and cooperation see
also Philip Slater's incisive, provocative little book, *The Pursuit of
Loneliness: American Culture at the Breaking Point* (Boston, 1970), especially pp. 5–7 and all of chap. 5. The best treatment of the revival
of joy in the religious life is Harvey Cox's *The Feast of Fools: A Theological
Essay on Festivity and Fantasy* (Cambridge, 1969); specific excerpts have
been taken from pp. 24–25 and 142ff. Also see Martin E. Marty and
Dean G. Peerman, *New Theology No. 8* (New York, 1971), pp. 6–7,
40–55. Cox's distinction between frivolity and festivity is similar to
Vance Bourjaily's discrimination between "black humor" and "gallows
humor," the latter being characteristic of the writing of Kurt Von-
negut, Jr. (see *New York Times Book Review*, 13 August 1972, p. 3).

Index